HEAVEN AND HELL WITHIN

notionpress.com

INDIA • SINGAPORE • MALAYSIA

HEAVEN AND HELL WITHIN

WHICH ONE DO YOU WANT?
KARMIC PERSONALITY DEVELOPMENT

HIMANSHU SHANGARI

notionpress.com

INDIA • SINGAPORE • MALAYSIA

Notion Press

No.8, 3rd Cross Street
CIT Colony, Mylapore
Chennai, Tamil Nadu – 600004

First Published by Notion Press 2020

ISBN 978-93-5206-206-5

ॐ

OM NAMAH SHIVAAY

This book has become possible with the Grace of Lord Shiva and each valuable word in it is due to his blessings.

Om Namah Shivaay

CONTENTS

They Come First

After bowing to Lord Shiva, let me take this moment to bow to the person who has been a very strong and supportive influence in my life. She is my respected and adorable mother, **Smt. Jeewan Lata**. So much can be said about her contribution to my life, that a whole book can be written about it. However, I will simply say that even an ocean of words can't describe her true contribution to my life.

After that, I bow to my dear and respected father **Lt. Sh. Bodh Raj Shangari**. Though he left us when I was nine only, the mere fact that he along with my mother brought me to this world, makes me indebted to him for this life as well as for the lives to come. God bless your soul father, wherever you are! Though you are physically not with me, you are always there with me and in me, through all the sweet memories of my childhood, and you will always be.

PRELUDE

So many books have been written on the topic of personality development that some people may think there is no need for more books. In reality, we need more and more books on this topic. This is because if each book is able to give you even one valuable tip to improve yourself which you didn't know before, the purpose of writing and reading the book has been served.

Human race is ever evolving. With continuous evolution, new researchers come up with new ideas and theories in various spheres of life, from time to time. Though many of them don't seem to deny theories established before their time, they add new values to the already existing theories so that we may benefit more from such theories.

However, some researchers do come up with new theories related to various spheres, from time to time. They offer information that was earlier not available to many. This is because a theory that holds good today may not hold equally good 100 years later, as with change in time and circumstances, the meanings and applications of various theories may change. Hence research and new information is the backbone of the process of evolution.

Personality development is a vast and complex sphere, as there is much more to it than appears on the surface. In order to improve yourself, you should first learn what lies inside of you, since it's easy to change something when you know what it is. This book has two sections. The first section deals with understanding of the conscious mind, subconscious mind, the aura; and transfer of energy through karmas, people and places.

The second section deals with habits and traits which may cause problems. Root cause of each habit/trait is discussed first. After that, approach as well as practices which can help in getting rid of such habit have been discussed. Various people may seem to suffer from the same problem from the outside, but the causes may be different for different people. Hence remedies should be applied after knowing the cause in each case.

For example, though various people may suffer from headache, the causes may be different. Headache may be caused because of high blood pressure, low blood pressure, hangover, lack of sleep, being hungry for a long period of time, stress and some other reasons. Though the visible effect seems to be the same which is headache, the treatment may be different depending on the cause.

Hence when you know the root cause of a problem, it is easy to fix such problem. For remedies, such practices have been mentioned which may not be much difficult to engage in and which at the same time, may not demand many resources. So learn which negative habits/traits you have and start working to fix them.

Lord Shiva Bless You

Himanshu Shangari

Section 1

Unveiling the Deepest Secrets

The Power and Illusions of Mind

A building was being constructed. Dozens of labourers were working hard to complete the task. It was a very hot day and the Sun was beating down hard. All the labourers seemed troubled from brutal attack of harsh sunlight and heat.

Three labourers were breaking big stones into smaller ones in harsh sunlight. All three of them seemed exhausted and they were soaked in sweat. A man went to one of the three labourers and asked him, "How are you, brother?"

The worker burst out angrily and said, "This is one hell of a life, Sir. I have to work hard in this heat and at the end of the day; all I get is Rs. 100 which my family will spend fast. Then they will ask me to go through all this again. Life is hell and it can't get worse than this."

This man went to the second labourer and asked him the same question. The labourer replied, "I am just about alright, Sir. Though I have to work hard all day long, at the end of the day the contractor pays me Rs. 100 which is sufficient to fulfill my family's needs. Hence I work hard and I get rewarded. Life is not very good but it is fair."

The man went to the third labourer and asked him the same question. He smiled with gratitude and said, "I am very well, Sir. God has been very kind to me. The structure we are raising is the building for a school. Once it gets ready, thousands of children will be educated and they will then shape the future of our country. I am very thankful to God that he chose me to be a part of this noble deed. Look at his grace that I am even being paid Rs. 100 every day for doing this noble deed. This money takes good care of my family. I couldn't ask more from life, Sir. Life is simply as good as it can get."

The man asking the question was a saint and he had brought some of his disciples to teach them an important lesson in life. He turned towards his students and said, "You see, heaven or hell, is only a point of view and nothing else."

Through resources matter, sometimes to some extents and sometimes to great extents, happiness never completely depends on resources. All the resources in the world are physical. Hence they can deal with the physical realm only. Happiness is not a state of physical body and it is a state of mind. Therefore, whether or not you are truly happy, depends on the type of mindset you have.

A positive mind finds reasons to be happy and content, even in the worst of the circumstances whereas a negative mind finds one thing or another to complain about, even in the best of the circumstances.

Hence it all starts with mind and it all ends with mind. If you have a positive mind which is capable of seeing beauty in all species and things created by nature and by man, you'll be able to enjoy most of your life. On the other hand, if you have a negative mind and you're good at finding faults with most species, things and situations; almost nothing can make you happy for long. This is because even if you are happy for some time, it is certainly short lasting happiness. Very soon, you will find reasons to complain about such state of happiness also.

Different people react differently in various circumstances. Depending on their mindsets and reactions towards situations, the results are also different for them. A positive mind gets something good out of every situation, whereas a negative mind fails to gain even from the best situations, in most cases.

People with negative mindsets start apprehending bad things right from the start. They have fears while entering into jobs, taking exams, entering into relationships and other things. Accordingly; they fail at most of them. Their negative minds ultimately make their fears come true. Then they may be found saying: "I felt it right from the beginning and look, it has happened!" In reality, it is only their fears and negative mindsets which have made such negative situations become reality.

On the other hand, there are people who have positive mindsets. They are confident that whatever is going to happen to them, whoever is going to come into their lives, they will gain from everything and everyone in the long run. Surprisingly, but not surprisingly; they gain a lot in their lives. They can get positive results even from seemingly negative situations and the reason is the same, the power of their minds.

It is the unmatched power of the human mind which when works in positive direction, can create strongly positive people who can make almost anything possible. On the other hand, if it works in negative direction, it can create strongly negative people who may fail even in the most positive circumstances. Hence good and bad, success and failure; all of them are ultimately controlled by the mind. Therefore, it becomes very important to recognize the power of mind and start making positive use of it.

Let's go deeper and see how the mind can create big successes or failures, depending on the direction it takes. In order to understand this concept, we'll need to see how the mind controls all your reflexes and actions, which even you don't know that it does. A part of your mind is called the subconscious mind and this is the part which is responsible for all the positivity and negativity that you have carried forward from your previous lives.

It is also referred to as unconscious mind. Subconscious mind forms more like the upper layers of this section of mind whereas the innermost layers may be referred to as the unconscious mind. For the sake of convenience, we'll refer to this entire section as subconscious mind throughout the discussion. The other part of your mind is the conscious mind, which you deal with in your sane senses. The subconscious part is much bigger and accordingly much more powerful than the conscious part of the mind.

When you try to create or do something, it is first created in the conscious mind and then the message is forwarded to the subconscious mind. Looking at a negative-minded person, as he starts creating stronger and stronger conscious negative thoughts about a specific thing or person, his conscious mind sends these thoughts to his subconscious mind. A time comes when the latter starts working more and more to make it happen. This process is so subtle that even the affected person may not feel that he is himself responsible for his failures and setbacks. Once the subconscious mind gains more and more strength through his negative ideas, it starts controlling the body, brain, speech and all other important functions of this person in a way which may finally produce the results desired by him, and he fails.

Hence when a positive and fruitful situation comes to him, his subconscious mind sends strong signals that this opportunity is not the right one and it should be passed. Since the subconscious mind is much stronger than the conscious mind, he passes on this opportunity under pretext of fear, apprehension, confusion, lack of confidence and other such feelings.

On the other hand, whenever a negative opportunity comes, his subconscious mind sends strong signals to him, telling him that this is the opportunity he should take. The subconscious mind does so because negativity and loss was fed to it by the conscious mind. Accordingly, the subconscious mind tries to make it come true. Needless to say, the person fails and the task given by him to his subconscious mind is completed by it.

Let's look into the working of a positive mind. A positive person creates positive thoughts and ideas in his conscious mind again and again. As these ideas are fed to his subconscious mind through the conscious mind, the former starts working to make them come true. In this case, when a negative opportunity comes to him, his subconscious mind sends strong signals that this opportunity should be avoided. Accordingly, he may not take it up.

On the other hand, when a positive opportunity comes to him, the subconscious mind sends strong signals that this is a perfect opportunity and he must take it. He simply follows the subconscious mind, he takes on the opportunity and the result is success. Once again, the subconscious mind has made the same thing happen in reality, which was fed to it. This is how the subconscious mind works: sending strong positive or negative signals to you.

You may have felt a strong sense of intuition or gut feeling, without knowing the reason behind it. These are the signals that your subconscious mind sends to you. Since you may not know the working of the subconscious mind, you may interpret them as gut feelings or intuitions whereas they may be nothing but your subconscious mind in action.

You may have faced situations, met people or seen places that give you feelings of Déjà vu which means they look like they have already happened to you, or they may seem familiar to you, but you don't know why. This is again your subconscious mind sending strong signals to you that this thing, place or person is familiar, since the subconscious mind has already dealt with it or something like it in one of your previous lives, very likely in your recent past life. Accordingly, you feel that this situation or person is familiar. Since you can't read the subconscious mind, it feels like Déjà vu to you.

The conscious mind is the part of your mind which interacts with you and your body on various levels. Everything fed to this part of the mind and everything coming out of it can be actively felt and understood by you. For example, when you drink juice, your tongue sends taste signals to your mind. Your mind tells you if it tastes good or bad and you know every detail of this act right from the beginning till the end. This is your conscious mind and almost all functions as well as activities of the conscious mind are within your knowledge. Hence this part of your mind is easy to understand.

Moving on to the subconscious mind, it is much more complex. The subconscious mind deals with your present life as well as with your past lives. In some cases, it deals more with the past life or lives than it deals with the present life. These are the cases that cause affected people to behave in ways which may seem strange to an average person. In reality, it is nothing but a shade of complex pattern of the subconscious mind.

The subconscious mind is that part of your mind which stores knowledge, information, memory and experiences from your present as well as past lives. Right from the first life of every soul, the subconscious mind starts storing and recording everything and life after life, it keeps doing the same. You can consider it like a hard disk which has tons of storage space and it can store vast amounts of data.

Since all the data from your past lives is recorded on your subconscious mind, and this data includes good and bad experiences, all success and failures, all wisdoms and follies from your past lives, the subconscious becomes very powerful. This is because it has already dealt with most situations in one or another of your past lives. Hence it knows much better what would be the right thing to do in a particular situation, as a situation that you think you are facing for the first time in your life may be nothing new for your subconscious mind. Your subconscious mind has all the records and this fact makes it a very powerful entity.

Let's try to understand this concept by going back to the beginning which means the first life form of a soul. Let it be your soul. As the soul assumes a physical body, it also gets various planes and entities. The first one is the physical plane which deals with physical affairs. The second one is the mental plane which deals with intellect, learning and other likewise things. The third one is the emotional plane which deals with feelings, emotions and experiences. The fourth plane is the astral plane which deals with conscience and through it; it deals with entities having higher or much higher consciences.

Apart from that, you also have a mind; broadly divided in two sections. The first section is called the conscious mind. The conscious mind is the active part of mind and it controls all the activities that you consciously go through. For example, if you try to learn a language, you're using your intellect to learn it and you are learning it consciously which means with visible effort. Likewise, if you go through some physical or emotional experiences; you do so consciously.

The second section of the mind is called the subconscious mind. Whatever you learn and/or experience through physical, mental, emotional and astral plane on conscious level; such information is stored on this section of your mind. Since it is your first birth, the subconscious is completely empty. As you start passing on instructions, experiences, information, choices and various other such things to it; it starts recording them.

The subconscious conducts various tasks. The first one is that it stores all the information sent by you to it through the conscious mind. Apart from that; it makes such information available to the conscious when needed, it executes tasks on its own, it sends warning signals, it gives gut feelings of liking/disliking and it does many other tasks. The subconscious does so on the request of your conscious mind only and the former doesn't have a wish of its own.

Since this is your first birth, the subconscious is empty. As you start going through experiences and as you start storing them on your subconscious with different tags attached to them; it becomes active and it starts doing its job. Taking an example; you feel hungry, you see animals or birds around you eating and you also decide to eat. As you eat, you feel satiated. Hence the conscious mind sends information to the subconscious that whenever hungry, you should eat something.

As you do so again and again, this information becomes a pattern as well as a command. The subconscious is a creature of habit. Whatever you send to it repeatedly, it starts executing such instruction on its own, based on the information fed to it. Hence your subconscious starts reminding you of food whenever the feeling of hunger strikes you.

When you try different food items like various types of fruits, vegetables and animals; you like some of them and you dislike some others. Such likes and dislikes are also stored on the subconscious. It means if you repeatedly liked apple and disliked guava; this information is stored on the subconscious. Hence it'll start giving you vibes of dislike when you see a guava whereas it'll start giving you vibes of like when you see an apple. All other eating priorities are set in this way.

Taking another experience, a lion attacks you but you escape; or it attacks someone else and it kills him. You witness this experience and you consciously decide that lion is harmful for you. This information is stored on the subconscious. Hence it starts warning you to stay away from lions. Likewise, you come across dogs and horses; and they behave friendly towards you. This information is also fed by the conscious to the subconscious. Hence the latter starts giving you feelings of like; when you see dogs or horses.

This way, all other likes and dislikes as well as dos and don'ts are stored on the subconscious and it starts executing them. It means memory is built. Without this memory, you'll have no idea that a lion attacked you once and you had a narrow escape. As a result, you may try to get closer to a lion or you may try to ignore its presence the next time you see it; and you may end up getting hurt. Hence the subconscious stores information provided by the conscious and it acts upon such information.

You meet and interact with people; and you record your experiences with them through the conscious mind. Such experiences are stored on the subconscious and it starts guiding you, based on those experiences. Hence you start recognizing that a particular person is good for you whereas another one is bad for you. Accordingly, you tend to be in the company of the first person more whereas you tend to avoid the second person.

Likewise, all other experiences are recorded on the subconscious. When you encounter wild animals or hostile people; you may learn and store a variety of things. For example, you may set a priority that some specific types of animals and people should be avoided as they have the potential as well as tendency to harm you. However when it is not possible to avoid them as they may attack or try to harm you anyways; you may try to defend yourself and in the process, you may counterattack. Hence you learn through such experiences that if you're not able to avoid them; you should counterattack.

These preferences are also stored on the subconscious and your defence mechanism is built. It means when you come across a lion or a specific person the next time; you may be prepared for two options. The first one is to avoid facing the lion or the person and if the circumstances don't allow doing so, you are prepared to counterattack.

You keep going through more and more experiences; and all of them are stored on the subconscious. You learn to appreciate beauty, develop specific tastes, recognize the opposite gender as well as your attraction for it; and all this information is stored on the subconscious. Hence the next time you see a female (considering you're a male), your subconscious may give you feelings of liking for her. As a result, you may try to pursue her and be with her.

This process continues till your death. You learn a lot and you store it on your subconscious mind. Then you die and the soul leaves the body. When that happens; the conscious mind dies with the body whereas the subconscious goes with the soul. Each soul gets only one subconscious mind throughout its journey and such subconscious never leaves it. On the other hand, you get a new conscious mind, each time you assume a physical body. Hence the body as well as the conscious mind dies whereas the soul as well as the subconscious survives.

With time, you get a new body as well as a new conscious mind. This is where things start to become tricky. In your first life, both the conscious and subconscious mind were playing for the first time; where the duration of one play is a lifetime. Hence your stored information on the subconscious mind through the conscious mind and the former released such information as and when needed. You were not surprised by such information because you remembered storing it.

It means when the subconscious gave a feeling of fear upon seeing a lion; you knew why this feeling was there. You suffered injuries through an attack by a lion and you had conscious memory of that incident. Hence you could relate to this feeling of fear, since your first conscious mind stored this information on the subconscious and the information was released to the same conscious mind. Hence you knew the source of this information and you were not confused. Likewise, the subconscious guided you in many other cases also; and your conscious had no problems relating to the instructions since the conscious itself stored them on the subconscious.

As you assume next body and a new life begins; things start getting complicated. You see a lion and your subconscious gives you a feeling of fear. However, you may not understand this feeling now. This is because the conscious mind which stored this information on your subconscious mind is not there any longer. This is a different conscious mind and it doesn't relate to this feeling. It means the first conscious mind was fine with this information since it had stored such information on the subconscious and it knew the source.

However, the second conscious mind knows nothing about the source of this information and hence it gets confused. A feeling of fear is there but you or let's say your conscious mind doesn't know why. Hence you may choose to go against this feeling and face a lion. If you choose to do that; you may suffer and two things may happen. Firstly, you store fresh information on the subconscious that lions are dangerous. Secondly, you realize that though you don't know the source of the information provided by the subconscious, it was correct.

Since you may not know what conscious as well as subconscious mind is; you may simply call it gut feeling or inner voice. Hence you learn that there are voices inside you which try to guide you from time to time. Though you may not know the source of such voices; they may come true in many cases. Your conscious mind may be confused whether to follow them all the time or not. This is because the conscious mind is all about active control. Hence it is comfortable relating to things/people when it can define their sources. However, it is uncomfortable with things/people of undefined origins.

This is where a clash in your personality may begin. The subconscious may suggest you a number of things but you (your conscious mind) may not be comfortable following them; since you don't know the source or reason. Life goes on. You learn a lot in this life also, you store such information on the subconscious mind and then you die. Here again, your subconscious as well as your soul leaves the body and they may set out on the journey to get a new body. The conscious mind dies with the body. It means that all the information stored by it is still there on the subconscious mind; but you are going to have a new conscious mind in the next life.

When you're born again; you get SM1 (subconscious mind number 1) whereas you get CM3 (conscious mind number 3). Life begins and you start storing information on SM1 through CM3. In this life, your SM1 has information stored by CM1, CM2 and CM3. Accordingly, it tries to release such information in order to guide you, based on your instructions only; given by CM1, CM2 and CM3. However, your conscious mind (CM3) doesn't recognize such information released by SM1, which was stored by CM1 and

CM2. Hence the confusion deepens in this life, compared to the second life.

This goes on life after life and suppose in the present life; you're operating with SM1 and CM1000. It means this is your birth number 1000. Hence you have had a thousand conscious minds so far; and you have stored information through them; on the very same subconscious mind, SM1. It means your subconscious mind has experiences of about a 100 thousand living years through the 1000 lives that you have had so far. In comparison, your conscious mind has experiences of about 35 years; considering you're 35.

As you can see, there's a world of difference between the knowledge possessed by SM1 and CM1000. This is where the confusion may get very strong. SM1 may release pieces of information from any of your previous lives and CM1000 may choose not to follow many of them since it doesn't know the sources. In this case, the net outcome is more dependent on your conscious mind which forms the active core of your personality.

It means if you have an accepting type of personality, you may choose to pay attention to what your subconscious says in most cases. Hence it may guide you to try a thing or a job, you may not know why but you may choose to go with the suggestion. As you do that; you may perform very well and you may discover that you are naturally gifted in such field.

In the deepest sense, there is no such thing as a natural gift and everything has to be earned. It only means that you had engaged in such field time and again in your past lives; very likely in your recent past lives. Let's say this field is that of dance. Your subconscious guides you to try it, you give it a try and sooner than you know; people recognize you as a gifted dancer. Though people may think you're a gifted dancer, it may not be so.

It means you learnt to dance in your past lives and you took it to the level of perfection; in your recent past life. Through lives and lives of experiences; your subconscious is filled with knowledge related to dance. Since you liked it a lot; the subconscious encourages you to try it; whenever an opportunity presents itself. You listen to it, you give it a try and the rest happens magically.

The magic happens because you already know all there may be to know about dance. Hence you start dancing like an expert though you've not learnt it in this lifetime. People call you gifted or they say you have natural talent for dance; but now you know the real reason. Likewise, the subconscious may guide you in thousands of other domains; based on the information you stored on it; during your previous lives; through various conscious minds.

The subconscious mind may be considered as a multiuser computer network which stores information on it. Though thousands of user can log into it and they can store information on it; they can only retrieve and change information that they actively stored. It means they may not access/change the information stored by other users. This system may be considered as the subconscious mind and the users may be considered as the conscious minds. The system has the information stored by all these users. However, each user may have active access to that information only, which he stored by logging into his profile.

Taking another example, suppose a bank offers facility for safety deposit boxes or lockers. Suppose it has 1000 boxes in a secure room. It means 1000 different users may use these lockers to store information/valuables in them. Though each user may access, retrieve and change what he stores; he may not do the same in case of lockers possessed by other users.

Though this room or network of lockers has information stored by 1000 users; each user has access to information stored by him only. The room may be considered as the subconscious mind and each individual user may be considered as a conscious mind.

Hence when you access your locker or your network account; you know that there are many other lockers or accounts in the same place. Such place has all the information but you have limited access to it.

Suppose someone has a master password to such computer network or he has a master key which can open all the lockers. In this case, he has access to all the information stored by all the users. Obviously, this person has much more information or valuables than each individual user, since he possesses the sum total of what each one of them possesses individually. This is the subconscious mind.

The subconscious mind operates like a network of users does; with some changes. For example, it may from time to time release such information to an active user; which he didn't store but which at the same time may be useful. The user can't relate to this information since he has no conscious memory of storing it. Hence he may choose to use it or ignore it. The system or the subconscious mind knows this information is valuable and it may help the user. Hence a lot of confusion may happen; as the subconscious may keep releasing information and the conscious may feel uncomfortable acting upon it, since it can't locate the source of such information.

Let's take another example. Suppose you meet a woman. As you interact with her, you start feeling an invisible bond with her, apart from the general physical attraction between the opposite genders. Hence you get voices from inside that you can trust this woman and she means well for you, though you may have met her only for 2-3 times. Your conscious mind may tell you to proceed with caution but the inner voices may tell you to move ahead without any fears. Though this woman may not give you any conscious reasons to believe or trust her at this stage; you may still get pulled to her due to such inner voices. Hence you may choose to trust her and you may develop a very good relationship with her; which may even turn into marriage.

The inner voices are the messages from the subconscious. Though you haven't met this woman before, in this life; you've been with her in your recent past life or more than one past life. Hence your subconscious recognizes her subconscious as well as her aura. Just like you, she also has the same subconscious but a different conscious mind. Hence she may also feel the same invisible pull towards you and things may progress fast.

Your aura is the outward expression of the sum total of all the energies stored on your subconscious mind. These energies include your desires, resolutions, preferences, habits, karmic energies, experiences and other energies. In other words, your aura is the outward expression of the net energy equation on your subconscious mind at any given point in time.

The way your conscious mind tries to recognize this woman is through any conscious experiences with her in this life; since the conscious can't go beyond this life. However, the way your subconscious tries to recognize this woman is by identifying her subconscious mind as well as her aura. Since her subconscious mind as well as aura is the same that she had in past life; though they may have undergone some changes; your subconscious recognizes her.

Hence for your conscious mind, she may be a woman you just met. However for your subconscious; she's the one you spent one or more than one of your past lives with. Your subconscious minds have developed utmost trust for each other and they are filled with love and respect for each other. Hence your subconscious may tell you again and again to trust her completely, since it vividly remembers beautiful experiences of a lifetime or lifetimes that you two have had together in the past.

Therefore, it encourages you and if you proceed; you may find that your gut feeling was absolutely right. When an actual thing like 'love at first sight' happens; it happens due to the same reason. When you strongly feel like someone is your soulmate, it may also happen for the same reason. You've been with this person a lot in your past life or lives. Hence your subconscious recognizes her at once and it gives you a strong go ahead signal.

Looking at it from another angle, suppose you love a woman and you two get married. Suppose the marriage goes very well and towards the end of your lives; both of you have developed a lot of love, affection, understanding, trust and respect for each other. It is natural that both of you may create strong conscious desires for being with each other, in the next lives also. Looking at another option, you may simply have desires to be with each other. With this common desire and with so much love, affection, understanding, respect and trust for each other, both of you die eventually.

When this mutual desire to be with each other is this strong; the system of nature may put it on priority. Hence both of you may be born again during the same timelines. Circumstances may introduce you and both of you may feel strong attraction towards each other. This attraction is nothing like the average physical attraction and it is much more than that. As you meet; the relationship may grow very strong in a short period of time and before you know; you two may get married. You may have that feeling of 'love at first sight' or 'she's my soulmate', in this case.

In reality, you've spent an entire life with her; loving, respecting and trusting her; and she has also done the same. Hence your conscious mind may not find reasons to trust her blindly, since it has no memory of those experiences. However, your subconscious may push you more and more towards her as it knows for sure that she's one of the most trustworthy persons for you, in the entire world. This inner voice is not based on some random wishful thinking; it is backed by solid experiences of a lifetime or more with this woman. This is why you feel like some people may be trusted though you have not interacted much with them.

Looking at this situation from another angle; suppose you're meeting a woman in this life and it is the first time with her; for your conscious as well as subconscious mind. It means you have had no interaction with this woman in any of your past lives. In such case, you may not hear many or any voices form inside, since your subconscious has no data related to her. Hence you'll need to depend on your conscious mind.

Accordingly, things may proceed slowly. You may take longer or much longer to like her if that happens. The same may happen with her also, when it comes for her to like you. The relationship may grow far slower in this case and entities like love, respect and trust may take long or very long to establish.

In the first case, the feelings may be very strong right from the beginning whereas in the second case, they may build up gradually over time. You have a well-established equation with the woman in the first case whereas you have no equation with the woman in the second case. Hence you have to start from the scratch in the second case. Accordingly, there may be no love or strong feelings of trust in the beginning phase; and such feelings may take time to build. As the number of good conscious experiences increases; love, trust and respect may start building. It means you're trying to accomplish with this woman; what you have already established with the other woman in your past life.

Likewise, all other experiences related to your physical, mental, emotional and astral plane are stored on your subconscious mind. Taking an example, suppose you died in a fire incident in your recent past life. Since the fire may have caused you a lot of suffering before you died; such suffering may leave strong impressions on your subconscious. As the impressions are fresh and strong; you may be scared of fire in this life. Though you may not consciously recognize the reason and you may find it odd; it makes perfect sense, since you've been recently burnt to death by it. Given the scale of age of your subconscious mind; 50 or 100 years count as recently.

In the same way, if you died by drowning in water in your recent past life; you may be scared of water bodies like lakes and rivers. The reason is the same. Your subconscious mind is trying to protect you by keeping you away from water, as it fears that you may drown again. Likewise, all other good and bad experiences you had in your past lives; shape up your subconscious mind in specific manners. As you're born and you live your present life; the experiences of this life make additions/modifications to the already recorded experiences. This process continues life after life; your subconscious keeps gaining more information; and it may also witness some modifications which have been consciously made by you.

For example, if you're afraid of water due to past life experiences, you may make modification to this memory. You may choose to face this fear. Hence you may learn to swim and devote a decent amount of time to this practice. Though you may be very much afraid in the beginning; such fears may start fading away with time and in a matter of some months or years; your fear of water may be gone.

It means you've made modification to one particular piece of information or memory stored on your subconscious mind. At the beginning of your present life; it told you to be afraid of water, based on the experiences of the past. However, you changed that piece of information with your conscious efforts. Hence it may not send warning signals when you get closer to water bodies. On the contrary, it may give you feelings of joy since you may have developed passion for swimming and the same passion has been recorded on your subconscious mind.

We have reached a very important point in discussion. This example shows that though your subconscious mind may have thousands of times more information than your conscious mind; it has no way of creating new information or modifying existing information on its own. On the other hand, your conscious mind may have far less information compared to the subconscious; but it is capable of recording new information and modifying existing information recorded on the subconscious. It means all the habits and patterns are stored on the subconscious and only the conscious mind can change them or introduce new habits or patterns.

Though a specific conscious mind like CM1000 can't directly access those sections of the subconscious which store information recorded by other conscious minds; there are still ways to make the subconscious release such information. The subconscious is all about repetition and patterns. Hence more conscious commands you send to it through repeated actions, thoughts, resolutions and desires related to a specific goal; more interested it may become in helping you out. It should be noted that we identity ourselves by our conscious minds since we have control over this part of the mind only. Hence when the word 'You' is mentioned, it means your conscious mind. Though we're much more than our conscious minds; many people may think they're represented by their conscious minds alone.

As you create a desire and as you start working for it more and more; you start sending signals to your subconscious, asking for help. The subconscious may be slow or very slow to respond; depending on some factors. The first factor is the strength of your conscious messages. It means if all you do is keep wishing for something to happen and you don't engage in efforts; the subconscious may not attach much importance to such signals.

Through thousands of lives of experiences; it understands that when you really want to achieve something, you work hard for it. Hence thinking or wishing alone may not do the trick and you'll need to engage in efforts. As you engage in more and more efforts in order to achieve a goal; you send stronger and stronger messages to the subconscious and it may come to your help.

The second factor deals with the fact how old the information in question is. For example, if you were an actor in your past life and you wish to achieve success in the same field in this life also; not much convincing may be required. This information is fresh and the subconscious may not have to dig deeper in order to get it out and release it to you. If you were an actor 5 lifetimes ago and you wish to be an actor again, the job becomes relatively difficult.

This is because the information about how you achieved success in acting is stored on relatively deeper layers of your subconscious mind; and a lot of information has been stored after that; in the 5 lives that followed. Hence as you try harder and harder on conscious level to achieve success, the same may be noted by your subconscious mind and it may start digging deeper and deeper. It may take more time in this case; but the subconscious may release many secrets and tricks with the passage of time.

If you were an actor 50 lifetimes ago and you wish to be an actor in this life also; the job becomes much more difficult. In this case, you may need to work even harder. The harder your conscious mind works; stronger signals it sends to the subconscious for help. Stronger are the signals received by the subconscious, deeper it digs. Deeper the subconscious digs; better are the chances of it releasing the required information to you.

As more and more of such information is released, you may realize that your potential as an actor has increased a lot.

Apart from that; you may notice that you're becoming more and more aware about the dos and don'ts of the showbiz. As a result, you may achieve more success.

Considering another application of the subconscious mind, whatever you store on it through the conscious mind, starts forming patterns which may be called habits. Taking an example, if you consciously choose to keep positive outlook on most things, you may continuously send signals of being positive to your subconscious mind. Likewise, if you consciously choose to give your best to the jobs at hand, the same may be recorded by your subconscious mind and it may also form a pattern.

Hence your subconscious may understand you as someone who's positive in approach and who won't quit. Then all of a sudden, you come across a situation or task which may look far bigger than you can handle and you may consciously get afraid of even attempting it or you may get confused whether or not you'll be able to succeed if you make an attempt. This is when your subconscious may come into play. It has loads of information stored on it and this information says you can do it. Hence you may end up attempting such task and completing it; though you were initially confused or scared.

Your subconscious keeps records of all your preferences, habits, desires, karmas and many other things. Since subconscious is a creature of habit and it is not capable of changing anything stored on it on its own; it tries its best to make you follow the already established patterns. In a situation like this, this trait of the subconscious may come as a blessing, since you may not have attempted this task without assurance from your subconscious.

You may have heard about the magic of positive thinking. Now you know how positive mindset works and why you should consciously engage in positive thoughts and actions. This is because all of them will be forwarded to your subconscious mind through your conscious mind. This is why wise people tell you to have positive attitude or positive mindset.

The same process works in the opposite direction also. For example, suppose you consciously doubt your chances of success in most jobs you attempt. Likewise, you consciously choose to quit most jobs which seem difficult or very difficult. This information is forwarded to your subconscious mind and with repetition over a period of time; it forms a pattern. Hence your subconscious mind may identify you as someone who's afraid of difficulties and failures.

Then one day, you face a situation where quitting is not an option and you have to succeed as it may be a do or die type of situation. Though you may try your best on conscious level; your subconscious mind may stand in opposition. In tune with the patterns formed by your conscious mind, it may keep scaring you that you are not capable of doing this job and you should quit. Hence your mind may get divided in two parts; with the bigger part telling you that you can't succeed. With this divided mindset, you may fail.

Though in both the cases; the subconscious seems to have the decisive edge, it is your conscious mind in reality, which holds the key. The subconscious may only give you what you've stored on it consciously. Whether such information helps you or it makes you fail; the subconscious has got nothing to do with that. It is a unit which stores, reminds and executes whatever the conscious mind has asked it to;

through repeated efforts and over a period of time. Hence you should choose wisely between positive and negative mindset; since it may ultimately decide your success or failure as well as happiness or sadness.

This is how the conscious and subconscious mind interact with each other and how they affect each and everything you do. Though the subconscious is much more powerful than the conscious in most cases; the former only does what the latter tells it to do. The only catch is that it takes a lot of time and effort for the conscious to create a pattern on the subconscious.

Once such pattern is formed; the latter starts executing it even if the former wants it to stop. If such is the case, the conscious needs to rewrite the unwanted pattern with effort and time. Once such pattern is replaced with a new pattern; the subconscious will start executing the new pattern. Hence choose wisely what you write on your subconscious since it is going to play an important role in each and everything you try to accomplish.

If you want your subconscious to give you courage and positivity; feed courage and positivity through repeated conscious efforts. If you want it to give you peace and optimism; don't feed disturbances and pessimism to it through repeated conscious efforts.

Working of Subconscious Mind and Aura

Human body contains 12 major energy centers within it. These energy centers are super microscopic, and they can't be seen even through the best of our microscopes. The job of these energy centers is to register, store and radiate energy.

These centers may contain various types of positive, negative and mixed energies which may have different strengths, different natures and different levels of activity. All the things that we do, our nature, our actions, our successes, our failures and all other things related to us are the resultants of the interactions of these energies within us. The subconscious mind contains the net equation of these energies and the aura is the outward expression of such equation.

At the time of birth of a person, different energies are registered in these centers. These energies may be called planetary energies and various other types of energies. These energies are active on the sky at the time and place of birth of a person. As soon as a baby comes out, these energies get registered with different energy centers within the body of this individual.

These energies are registered in various energy centers in different ways, depending on their strengths, positions and levels of activities at the time and place of birth of this individual. These combinations may be arranged in a way that some energy centers may register a number of strong energies, whereas some other energy centers may not contain much energy.

As soon as these energies are registered with different energy centers, they start interacting with other energies in the same energy centers as well as those in other energy centers. How many strong and how many weak, how many positive and how many negative energies are registered with various energy centers of your body is not coincidental. It is decided on the basis of your past life karmas, resolutions, desires, habits and experiences.

Whatever positive and negative energies you carried at the last moment of your past life, are forwarded to you at the beginning of present life. Suppose each one of these energies is taken as a variable likely x, y, z and their interactions give out a resultant equation at any point in time. Let's call it the net energy equation at any point in time. It means you get the same net energy equation at the beginning of this life, which you had during the last moment of your recent past life, in most cases.

This is because you need a physical body to make changes to this energy equation. Since you had no physical body between the time you died in your recent past life and you were born in this life; you couldn't make any changes to this equation on your own; during all this time. Though some specific people may make some changes to this equation on your behalf even when you don't have a physical body; such changes may not happen in most cases as those procedures are not even known to most people. Hence you may carry the same equation of energy at the beginning of this life, which you carried at the last moment of your recent past life.

It means when enlightened people say that death is nothing but sleep, it is true. Whatever energies you carry at the last moment of this life don't go away with death and they come back in the next life. Hence death indeed is sleep and you get all the same personality traits, desires, resolutions and other likewise things that you had at the end of your recent past life. It is like when you sleep every night, you wake the same next morning. This validates another theory of the enlightened ones; that the journey of soul is continuous and death is nothing but one of many stoppages on the way.

For this reason, the problem with negative mindset is not temporary. It has been there in past lives and it will be there in next lives as well. It won't go away on its own and it will stay until you start putting in conscious efforts to replace it with positive mindset. Then positive mindset will take its place and start being there for the rest of this life as well as for the coming lives, until you make conscious efforts to change it.

A question may arise that how the exact same equation of energy from the past life is transferred to a person, which he carried at the time of death in his previous life? The answer to this question comes in the form of time, date, month, year and place of birth of such person. A person who carried a specific equation of energy at the time of his death in his past life will assume his next birth only when the skies over the place of his birth reflect the exact same equation of energy. This equation will be transferred to him through energies in various energy centers in his body.

Since the net equation of energy over the skies of a particular place keeps changing, this is why even twins separated by a minute may be somewhat different from each other. This is because the net equation of energy changes in that minute and the person coming a minute later gets a different energy equation than the one coming a minute earlier.

This validates the need for a person to take birth at the exact decided place and at the exact decided time, because he has to carry the exact same energy equation which he carried at the end of his past life. Such exact same energy equation may be there; only at a certain specific place, date and time, once in many years.

For this reason, your next birth may be fixed in terms of place and time as soon as you die in this life. The net energy equation at the time of your death is calculated and accordingly, the next possible location and time for that energy equation to appear on the sky is also calculated. This may become your time and place of birth, if some other criteria are met. Since such criteria are beyond the scope of present discussion, we'll skip them.

You may have wondered why the best type of people like saints and gods as well as the worst type of people are born after longer periods of time. In other words, why are these people much less in numbers than average people?

This is due to the reason that such people whether positive or negative, carry rare types of energy equations. Once they leave their physical bodies, the next occurrences of the same energy equations may not appear soon. For this reason, these people are not as many in numbers as others are, since they have to wait for their exact energy equations to appear on skies, in order to be born.

By now we know that we start with the same energy equations in this life that we finished with, in our previous lives. We also know that the journey of soul and the equation of energy, whether positive or negative, are continuous.

Moving on, as different types of weak and strong, positive and negative energies have been registered in your body in various energy centers, they start interacting with one another. Accordingly, you are able to see various shades of behaviors in your personality. This is because at times, certain specific negative energies may dominate the equation. Accordingly, your behavior may become comparatively negative. At other times, certain specific positive energies may dominate the equation. Hence your behavior may become comparatively positive.

The outward expression of the sum total of all these energies at any point in time is called your aura. The net equation of energy has two forms to exist in. It exists in its basic form in your subconscious mind. When it gives an outward expression, such expression comes out in the form of aura. Hence aura is the outward expression of net energy equation, at any point in time.

Taking an example, suppose a star like our Sun is going through internal combustion. It produces heat through such combustion which may be going on within it. Based on its net energy equation at any point in time; it emits energy or to be precise, a specific equation of energy. When we see this equation of energy from outside, it is Sun's aura. If we're able to go inside the Sun and see this energy equation from the inside; it is Sun's subconscious mind.

Though the energy equation within a star as well as the one that comes outside is the same; the expression is different. The equation of energy in the subconscious is the inward expression of it whereas aura contains the outward expression of the same equation of energy. Hence your aura at any point in time reflects the net equation of energy formed in your subconscious mind. In other words, the subconscious is the contained form of aura whereas aura is an expressive form of the subconscious.

Apart from reflecting the net equation of subconscious mind, aura does other jobs also. It is a two way connection between the subconscious and the entire existence. Hence it gives out the net equations of energy contained in the subconscious at different points in time. At the same time, it transfers outward energies to the subconscious. Such transfer may depend on various factors which we'll discover later on.

It means your aura is your way of influencing other people and places with your net energy equation, as it keeps radiating such energy equation. Hence when you interact with a person, your net energy equation is radiated by your aura and it may influence the other person in many ways; depending on the type of equation you have, the type of equation he has and other factors. At the same time, your aura is your way of being influenced by other people and places, as it keeps receiving energy from these sources. Here again, what types of energies it receives and how much of those energies it receives are dependent on various factors.

It means your aura brings all good and bad things to you. Hence it becomes the most important factor in determining your success and failure. The aura can be changed with specific techniques and activities, and this is how we can turn the game to our advantage.

The energies contained in your aura interact with the energies present in the auras of various entities in the entire existence. Accordingly; various outcomes may appear, depending on the resultants of the interactions of your aura with those of different people and entities.

An aura is a collection of energies. Hence the term 'interactions with other auras' doesn't means physical interactions. It means that for the aura of one person to interact with auras of other people, physical interactions are not necessary, since energy can interact with other energies in many ways. For example, when you talk to someone over phone, your aura interacts with their aura though you are not physically interacting with each other. When you listen to a song, dialogues of a movie or speech; the auras of those in the song, dialogues or speech interact with your aura, through the medium of voice which carries their auras.

Similarly when you read something, like you are reading this book for instance, the aura of the author starts interacting with yours. The energy in this case is carried through the words. The types of interactions of aura such as listening to speech, songs, dialogues or reading text are one-way aura interactions in most cases. It means that through such interactions, the aura of the author, singer or actor can influence your aura, since it has a medium to reach you. However, your aura can't influence their auras, since you don't have a medium to send your energy to them. Hence you can receive but you can't transmit energy.

On the other hand, when two or more people talk to each other or they interact with each other in any other form, the auras of all these individuals interact with one another. Hence your aura tries to influence everyone else's aura through words, gestures and even through your mere presence at one such place. Likewise, their auras try to influence your aura through the same media.

Let's see how this interaction may affect your successes and failures. Suppose you want a job and you appear for an interview. As you appear before the person conducting the interview, your aura starts interacting with his aura.

When auras of two people interact with each other, various outcomes are possible. If both auras carry similar types of positive or negative energy equations, the outcome may be favourable. This is because a person carrying net negative aura generally tends to be impressed by another person carrying net negative aura. Likewise a person with net positive aura tends to be influenced by another person carrying net positive aura. There is a saying, 'Birds of a feather flock together'. This is true in case of auras; as a net positive aura prefers other positive auras, whereas a net negative aura prefers other negative auras.

If the aura of the person conducting the interview and your aura are in accordance, his aura may be favourably influenced. It means that he may be convinced and this may work well for you. If the aura of the interviewer is in opposition to your aura, your aura may repel his aura and you may fail.

Let's introduce more variables to this equation and see what may happen. Suppose 20 candidates appear for the same job, of which nine have auras in accordance with the aura of the interviewer and 11 have auras which repel the aura of the interviewer. It means that the interviewer may be impressed by 9 out of 20 people and he may not like 11 candidates.

Hence these 11 candidates may be given no consideration and accordingly they may not stand any chance for the job.

However, there is only one job and there are 9 candidates in accordance with the aura of the interviewer. In other words; the interviewer is impressed by all 9 candidates. This is the time to know that apart from having net positivity or negativity; auras have net strengths, just like energies from which they are made of. It means though 9 candidates have convinced the interviewer, the one whose aura is the strongest among them may influence the aura of the interviewer the most. Accordingly, he is likely to be the one who gets the job.

Likewise, this aura equation applies to every sphere of life. Taking another example, suppose a boy and girl meet. Instantly, their auras start interacting with each other. The boy may ask the girl out. If the aura of the boy is in accordance with the aura of the girl, her aura may be positively influenced by his aura. Hence the inner feeling of the girl may start telling her that she likes this guy. On the other hand, if the aura of the boy is not in accordance with girl's aura, the answer may be negative.

Let's introduce more variables to this equation. Suppose many boys meet this girl at a place and out of them, there are 4 whose auras positively influence her aura. It means the girl may choose to continue with one of these 4. When it comes to choose one among these 4, the one whose aura influences her aura with maximum strength may be chosen by her.

Similarly, this theory can be used to explain other spheres of life and those ones also where you don't have to choose between many people that you like. For example, while making friends with someone, the simple aura rule that may apply is that if both the auras are in accordance, you are comfortable with this person and friendship may happen. Even if your aura is in accordance with 100 other people, you can become friends with them also, without losing the first friend or without having to choose just one. The concept of relative strengths of auras works well in this situation also and here is how.

Though you may have dozens of friends and auras of all these friends may match your aura type, the ones who have the strongest auras may become your best friends followed by the ones who have relatively weak auras. They may become your friends of second circle, followed by the third circle of friends and so on until you reach the outermost circle of friends. These are the people who you may call casual friends or you may simply be friendly with them.

Hence whether you want to impress a client, your boss, your girlfriend, your wife, your parents, your friends or anyone else; or you want to achieve something, your aura will always be a deciding factor. Your aura as well as subconscious mind is not stationary and they are changing continuously. As already discussed, you're born with a specific equation of energy stored on your subconscious mind. This equation radiates in the form of your aura. Hence you're born with a specific type of aura.

As you grow older and you develop thought patterns as well as conscious mindset; you start sending instructions to your subconscious mind. These instructions start making changes to the subconscious, where such changes may be positive or negative, based on the conscious instructions sent by you through your thoughts, actions and experiences.

Based on these instructions; the subconscious starts attracting various types of energies from the universe, through your aura. Suppose you're interested in a specific field of profession, say acting. You start putting more and more conscious effort when it comes to learn acting, act and keep yourself updated about the news related to this field. Over a period of time, your subconscious registers this pattern and it starts doing a number of jobs.

If you're taking an acting class, it'll motivate you to pay more and more attention. At the same time, it may help you with various things related to this field. For example, when watching TV, it may help you with better focus when you watch something related to the field of acting, compared to when you watch something else. Likewise, it may encourage you to engage in practices which enhance your acting skills and it may also make you engage in company of such people who may help you in this field.

Apart from that, it may start attracting people relevant to this field with more strength. It means your aura may try to influence more and more people related to this field so that you may begin your career and witness good results. Taking an example, suppose you're at a party where a number of important people related to movie and television industry are also present. Your aura may try to influence them in ways that they may be impressed by you.

For instance, a common friend of yours may introduce you to a producer and as you begin to interact with him; your aura may do its best to influence his aura. At the same time, your subconscious may send you more and more such information stored on it; which may help you impress this producer. Hence you may leave a good or very good visible impression on his conscious mind and at the same time, you may leave a good or very good invisible impression on his aura/subconscious through your aura/subconscious. This may help you get some work through him.

Taking another example, suppose you and various other artists are supposed to perform on stage turn by turn at an event which is being attended by some important people in movie industry. Suppose one of them is going to give you a chance in one of his future movies based on your performance at this event. Your aura may influence his aura in a way that he may not feel like leaving this event before your performance. Hence he may stay till you perform, he may watch you perform, he may get impressed and he may offer you a chance. Likewise, your aura/subconscious may help you in a number of other ways; depending on the strength and nature of patterns formed on it by your conscious mind.

Let's take a different example. Suppose you get interested in the field of spiritualism and you start putting more and more conscious effort in order to achieve spiritual growth. Hence you may watch relevant TV programs, listen to relevant audio discourses, read relevant books, interact with relevant people, attend to a number of relevant events and engage in various practices like meditation on your own. Over a period of time, your conscious mind may register a pattern on your subconscious and the latter may start helping you according to this pattern.

With time, your aura/subconscious may grow stronger in a specific manner. Hence it may start attracting spiritual entities or higher consciences spread throughout the existence. As a result, you may feel like you're being guided by some intuitions or some type of divine guidance from time to time. Stronger is the pattern registered on your aura and stronger as well more positive is your aura; more may be the quantum of such guidance received by you.

If you keep moving on this path; a time may come when you may feel that in order to do most things related to this field; you don't have to put conscious effort. Divine guidance may guide you through intuition, you may choose to follow and you may end up doing the right things. Liberation is the last stop on this path or it is the destination of this path. When you reach there; your subconscious may get connected to the universal conscience commonly known as God, through your aura.

Hence your subconscious may receive instructions from the universal conscience, it may forward them to you and you choose to act upon them. At this stage, there's no will of your own, which means you don't have any conscious will. Hence you operate through instructions given by your subconscious which receives such instructions from the universal conscience. Since you don't have a desire of your own and you're not engaging in any karma for fruits; you're liberated.

This is because only three things stop you from being liberated. They are; payback for bad karmas, rewards for good karmas and desires/resolutions to achieve things/ people. Since you don't have desires of your own; you're free from them. Since you don't engage in any karma for your own benefit as well as on your own will, you're free from good or bad results of such karmas. Even if you end up hurting or killing someone, guided by the universal conscience; such karma may not leave any impression on your subconscious. It means you may not be judged for such karma. This is because you have now become a medium or a tool and you don't have any wish of your own.

It is like people are punished for murdering other people but murder weapons never receive such punishments and they are not even judged. This is because we understand that they have no will of their own and they'll do whatever the ones possessing them wish. Hence a knife or a gun doesn't receive punishment for murder, since it is the medium and not the doer. Likewise, you become a medium through which the instructions of the universal conscience are carried out. Since you're merely carrying out such instructions without any conscious involvement at all, you're free from the results. Hence you're engaging in Nishkaam karmas (karmas without desires for results) and you're liberated. This topic is much more detailed than this. Hence we'll leave it here for the time being.

The same theory works in other direction also. It means if you consciously start disliking a thing or a field; your subconscious may register a pattern over a period of time. Hence it may discourage you from engaging in anything related to such field. At the same time, your aura may repel people related to such field so that they don't have good interactions with you or they don't have any interactions at all.

Likewise, if you feed more and more negativity to your subconscious through your conscious; it may register strong negative patterns over a period of time. When that happens; it may start repelling positive people, things and places; and it may start attracting negative people, things and places. Through them, it may receive even more negative energy. Hence your subconscious may become more negative and your aura may radiate more negativity. Such negativity may push positive people as well as opportunities away from you and it may bring negative people and opportunities closer to you. Hence you (your conscious mind) are the biggest factor when it comes to change the net energy equation of your subconscious/aura.

It means that though you may have no control over the type of net energy equation you get at the time of your birth, as you have no control over the past, you can change this equation positively or negatively through your conscious desires, resolutions, thoughts and actions. When it comes to change this equation; the time and effort needed to change specific parts of this equation may vary, depending on how strong such parts may be.

It means that stronger is a pattern registered on your subconscious, more conscious effort and time may be required to change/rewrite such pattern. Such pattern may have been created over a period of many years or even over a period of one lifetime or more. Hence you may have to put in sustained and dedicated conscious efforts over a period of years to change/rewrite such pattern. On the other hand, some patterns may be weaker and they may be changed with less conscious effort and time.

Whether this path is short, long or very long, there is no other path and this is the only path. Hence if you want to improve yourself, you have to start walking on this path. Regardless of the length of a path; you will reach your destination, if you keep walking on it. Hence if you wish to see better results in various spheres of life, you need to increase net positivity of your subconscious/aura.

It means you need to consciously engage in positive thought patterns, actions, desires and resolutions. When you do that, your subconscious shifts towards positivity and your aura is able to attract even more positivity from the universe. As your aura/subconscious gets more and more positive energy, it becomes capable of doing better things in various spheres of your life. Accordingly, you may become more successful, more loved and above all, a better human being.

Addition of Energy through Karmas

Energy is continuously added to your subconscious/aura through various types of karmas you engage in. Karmas can be broadly divided into three types; good karmas, bad karmas and neutral karmas.

Though it is difficult to achieve exact definitions for them, let's try to understand broader definitions for them. If you engage in an action, speech or thought with the intention of benefit of others, it is called good karma. If you engage in an action, speech or thought with the intention of hurting others, it is called bad karma. If you engage in an action, speech or thought with the no intention or desire, it is called a neutral karma.

It should be noted that a karma is decided by the intention and not by the expression. Let's try to understand this concept with the help of some examples. Suppose a criminal kills people for money. Since his primary motive is to earn money and he's killing people for this motive; these karmas are bad, since he's making other people suffer for his own benefit.

Suppose a police officer kills this criminal in an encounter. If this officer's intention is to do his duty and restore balance by killing the criminal, it is a good or neutral karma. However, if he's personally biased against criminals and he kills this one instead of arresting him, though the latter may be surrendering; it is a bad karma. In this case, the officer is not killing the criminal to restore balance or to do his duty; he's killing him to satisfy himself. Since he's taking human life for selfish motive, it's bad karma.

Suppose the officer arrests this criminal and the latter faces a trail. The judge punishes him with death penalty. If the judge has made this decision on merit and he's not biased against the criminal, it's a good/neutral karma. However, if the judge has personal bias against murderers and he goes out of way to ensure that the criminal is punished; it's a bad karma.

Taking another example, suppose your brother is in dire need of money, he asks from you and you give him such money. If your intention is to help him and strengthen the bond; it is a good karma. However, if you help him so that he may feel small in front of you for the rest of his life; it is a bad karma. If you help him and no good or bad intentions are there, it is a neutral karma. In this case, you're neither looking for reward nor for selfish motives. He needs money, you have it and you give it. That's all there is and the thought of doing good or the thought of gaining advantage doesn't cross your mind.

This type of karmas are rarely practiced since most people consciously or subconsciously look for rewards when they're helping others. Looking at conscious desire for fruits; you help your brother and you consciously wish for the rewards. For example, you may tell other family members and friends how you helped him. Your intention is to gain praise for this karma. Since you have conscious desire for fruit of this karma and you mean well for your brother; it is a good karma.

Looking at subconscious desire; you help your brother and expect that he'll respect you more or your bond may strength after this. Though you don't tell anyone about this, you may wish that he does so. It means you don't tell your family but if he tells them; they praise you and you feel happy. It means in this case, a subconscious desire is there for fruits. Hence it is a good karma.

Looking at neutral karma; you help him and the chapter is closed. You don't feel like telling anyone about this act. At the same time, you're not affected in any way if he tells other people and they praise you. This is a neutral karma. However, if you feel happy when others praise you for this karma, it's a good karma since you were subconsciously expecting these results.

Looking at another variation, if you feel embarrassed when they praise you and you even advise your brother not to tell anyone as you feel uncomfortable when people praise you for good deeds, it is not a neutral karma and it is a good karma. This is because the fruit of this karma is still affecting you. In the first case, it made you happy whereas in the second case, it embarrassed you.

The embarrassment may be there because you may be a very good person and you may think that getting praise or rewards for good karmas dilutes their goodness. Though you're noble in thinking so; a desire for fruit is still there. It means you're trying to increase goodness in you as well as protect it. Hence deep down; you've engaged in this karma in order to become a better person though you may not want any outside rewards at all. Hence this may be a good karma of the highest order but it is still not a neutral karma; since the desire for fruit is there, even if such desire is to become better as a person. Only if there is no desire and you're not affected by the outcome of this karma in any manner; it is a neutral karma.

Let's look at another scenario. Suppose relevant authorities of a country ask their soldiers to invade another country for selfish motives; and the soldiers also know this fact. If a soldier chooses to be a part of such invading unit; he's engaging in a bad karma. Though it may seem that he's only doing his duty like the police officer or the judge; it is not so in reality.

Whenever there is a clash between priorities; the higher ones should be saved. A person who serves government is bound by two obligations. The first one is his obligation to his job whereas the second one is his obligation to his conscience or himself. As long as his duty is in line with his conscience; he's engaging in good or neutral karmas, even if he's killing someone. However, if there's a clash between his conscience and duty; conscience takes priority. Hence if he chooses to harm others under pretext of duty by suppressing his conscience; it is a bad karma.

Looking deeper; the soldier knows that if he refuses to be a part of the attacking unit; he may lose his job. Since he may not want to lose this job; he may become a part of such unit. Hence deep down; he's doing it for job which means for selfish motive. It applies to all people working for governments when they face such choices. If they choose to harm the innocent in order to save their jobs; they may justify themselves by assuming that they were only following orders. However, they had the choice to leave jobs but not engage in such harmful acts. Since they preferred jobs over right or wrong; such karmas are bad. Hence the solider in question is engaging in a bad karma by choosing to be a part of such unit.

Let's look at this equation from a different angle. Suppose this army attacks and the country which is attacked engages in counterattack. The authorities tell their soldiers to fight and kill anyone who tries to invade. The soldiers follow and they may end up killing many enemy soldiers. One such solider is not engaging in bad karmas since his duty as well as conscience are in alignment. His conscience guides him to protect himself, his family and his land from foreign invasions and his country is also telling him to do the same.

It means the solider in this case is not killing to gain something but he's killing to protect his land and the people living there. Hence he's engaging in a good or neutral karma. If the solider has conscious or subconscious desires for fruits attached to this karma; it is a good karma. If such desires are not attached; it is a neutral karma. For example, if he wishes for medal, reward or praise; he's engaging in a good karma. On the other hand, if he doesn't have any desires and he simply does what needs to be done; he's engaging in a neutral karma.

Looking at another probability; suppose the invading army is defeated and they start running back. If a soldier in the defending army shoots at the running soldiers, he may be engaging in bad karmas. This is because he's justified in killing them as long as they pose direct threat to his land. Since the threat is removed, he may now be shooting at them for personal satisfaction or in order to avenge some fellow soldiers who may have been killed by the attacking army. Since the task has become personal and the motive is selfish; such karma becomes a bad one.

Considering another variation; suppose a fellow solider is seriously wounded and he's about to be captured by enemy soldiers. The soldiers of defending army may have set some codes for such situations and the soldier in question may find that the fellow solider is requesting him to kill the latter. The wounded soldier may realize that if he's captured, the enemy will make his life hell and they may also be able to get some secrets out of him. Hence he may request this soldier to kill him before he's captured. Seeing no option to save this fellow solider and seeing that a capture is inevitable now; he may shoot the fellow soldier.

In this case, the karma is good or neutral and not bad though it may look like a bad one. The key to decide the nature of a karma lies with intention. The intention of this soldier is to honour the request of a wounded companion who's begging the former to kill him, in order to be saved from torture and to avoid passing any sensitive information to the enemy. Since the soldier in question has nothing to gain from this situation and he's doing it for the wounded soldier; this karma is good or neutral. Here again; if such soldier has desires for fruits attached to it, like he may enjoy when other soldiers praise him for this act, the karma is good and not neutral. If he doesn't have any desire and he's not affected by the fruits of this karma; the karma is neutral.

Hence intention is the key to decide the nature of a karma. Accordingly, the intention and not the expression should be considered when trying to decide whether a karma is good, bad or neutral. This topic is vast and it can't be contained even in dozens of books. Hence we'll move forward, now that we have achieved basic clarity on the topic.

Good karmas add positive energy to the aura whereas bad karmas add negative energy to the aura. Through aura, such energy goes to the subconscious. Hence the net energy equation of the subconscious as well as the aura changes. Looking at neutral karmas; they add positive energy of different kind. This energy is spiritual and it doesn't attract materialistic benefits like an average type of good energy. Instead, it helps you get rid of desires. It means such energy helps you achieve liberation since liberation is the state of having no conscious desires.

Let's look at some basic examples of good and bad karmas; though their definitions may change in some cases, based on your intentions. When you help a poor man or offer service to a physically disabled person or an old person, you engage in good karmas. Likewise, when you treat an injured dog or a cat; or plant more trees so that the earth may become a better and cleaner place to live, you engage in good karmas. Such karmas add positive energy to your aura/subconscious.

On the other hand, when you rob another person or injure him for selfish motives; you engage in bad karmas. Likewise, when you rape someone, kill animals for selfish motives like for fun or you engage in acts of violence without having just reasons to do so; you engage in bad karmas. Such karmas add negative energy to your aura/subconscious.

Likewise, you can engage in good, bad or neutral karmas through speech and thoughts also. As a basic rule, karmas generated through actions are the strongest type of positive or negative karmas followed by those generated through speech, followed by those generated through thoughts or wishes. This rule holds well in most cases, though the order may be rearranged in some cases; depending on specific situations.

For instance, you may discourage, demotivate or curse someone so much that they may commit suicide. Though all you've done is engage in bad karmas through speech; this one is higher in quantum than many karmas falling in the physical action category. Likewise, you may encourage, soothe or heal someone so much through your speech or prayers that such karma may be higher in quantum than many karmas falling in the physical help category. Hence there is the basic rule and there are exceptions.

Though many of your thoughts and mind patterns involve you only; there are some specific types of activities of your mind which may be classified as good or bad karmas. For example, when you pray for the benefit of other people or species; and their benefits include your benefits also; such karmas may be good but not neutral since you wish to gain something in return. It is like your father is in hospital fighting death and you pray for him to recover. If such prayer is motivated by conscious or subconscious desires of your own profits or losses through his survival or death; such prayer may be good but not neutral. However, if you pray for him merely for his sake and no thought or feeling of your own profit or loss is there; such prayer is a neutral karma.

Likewise, if you pray for strangers or for some causes which don't bring any direct benefits or losses to you; it is a neutral karma. However, if desires for fruits are involved, such prayers may be good but not neutral. Suppose you're praying for an unknown immigrant whose case is under consideration for legal status in a country where you too are an immigrant without legal status. Since you know consciously or subconsciously that if he wins his case, it may help your case also; this prayer is not neutral.

Looking at the other side of the picture, any thoughts or thought patterns through which you wish bad for other people or species without just reasons; are bad karmas. For example, wishing that a person should fall ill or that something bad should happen to him so that he may not appear for a competition or a job interview and you may win the competition or get the job due to his absence, is a negative karma. This is because you try to send negative energy to this person through your mind so that he may be harmed and you may benefit.

All other thoughts and thought patterns of this type may be classified as bad karmas. They add negative energy to your aura and more negative energy means more troubles in future. On the other hand, good and neutral karmas add positive energies of their own brands to your aura/ subconscious.

Hence think positively, speak positively and engage in positive karmas. Doing so will add more and more positive energy to your aura/subconscious. Hence, if you spread more and more positivity around you, such positivity will find you and good things may start happening to you. On the other hand, if you spread more and more negativity around you through negative karmas; such negativity will find you and bad things may start happening to you. When they say, "Man is the maker of his own destiny", it is true. Whatever good and/or evil you create, it comes back to you. Hence choose your karmas wisely.

Let's see how good or bad karmas add positive or negative energy to the aura and change the net energy equation. Suppose there is a very old person who needs help to carry a bag back home from a place. You see the situation and you decide to help him out. The man accepts it and this is where the good karma and addition of positive energy to your aura start taking place.

As you start helping this person, he may start thinking or feeling positive about you. Though he may actually thank or bless you just one or two times, his mind may continuously keep thanking and blessing you. It means that his mind may initiate a process through which positive energy may be transferred from his aura to your aura. As a result, your aura may become comparatively more positive than it was, before helping this person or before receiving packets of positive energy from him.

Likewise, when you hurt someone, he may transfer negative energy through his aura to your aura. Such positive or negative energy is the reciprocation of good or bad karma done by you. In other words, this energy is reciprocation of good or bad energy sent by you to a person. Forces of nature make sure that this reciprocal positive or negative energy reaches you and it is added to your aura; whether your aura, conscious mind and even your subconscious mind wants to receive it or not.

This practice is supported by forces of nature in order to maintain balance of energy. Otherwise, the balance of energy in the universe may be disturbed, which may result in eventual collapse of the entire universe. For example, if a person keeps engaging in bad karmas, he keeps sending negative energy to others. When counteracting packets of negative energy from the other side reach him, he may always choose not to accept them, if he has a choice whether to accept them or not. Thus, he may keep harming others without any addition of negative energy to his aura. It means that he may keep hurting others and in return, he may not have to suffer.

If such things keep happening, more and more people may start engaging in negative karmas; and they may reject the resultant negative energies. Soon, only evil may prevail in the world as people may not be afraid of doing anything bad as they don't have to suffer the consequences. Accordingly the balance of universe may be disturbed and the theory of karma may fail completely.

Hence forces of nature ensure that if you do good or bad to someone, which means if you send positive or negative energy to someone, the reciprocating positive or negative energy is received by your aura and added to it, whether you want it or not.

Getting back to the example; as the old man you help sends packets of positive energy to you, these packets are received by your aura. Accordingly, this quantity of positive energy is added to your aura, making your aura more positive than before. As a result, you have comparatively better chances of achieving various types of good things in life. At the same time, you have comparatively fewer chances of falling victim to sufferings, losses and failures on various fronts of life, since your aura has become more positive. Accordingly, it may start repelling negative events and negative people with more strength. Though this small act of help may only result in small increase in net positivity of your aura, you are gaining positive energy and it is perfectly fine as long as you are gaining it, for this is what you need.

Let's see how energy is transferred by species other than human beings. The energy transfer works in a similar manner more or less. Animals and other species don't transfer positive or negative energy through their voices in all cases. However, their minds are capable of sending you positive or negative energy in response to your actions. Accordingly, your aura shifts towards positivity or negativity, depending on whether it has received positive or negative energy.

You may have noticed that when you help or hurt animals through your karmas, they make different types of sounds which come out in responses to your positive or negative actions. These sounds carry some amounts of positive or negative energies which are added to your aura. For example, when you feed a hungry dog, caress it or treat a wound on its body, you may notice that it releases a thankful type of sound. This sound carries packets of positive energy which target your aura, thereby making your aura more positive.

On the other hand, when you beat a dog with a stick or you inflict a wound on its body; you may find that the sound coming out of its mouth is different. This changed sound is the carrier of packets of negative energy which are added to your aura. With the addition of these packets of energy, your aura becomes comparatively more negative. This reduces the chances of good things happening to you and it increases the chances of you falling victim to sufferings or problems.

Such additions of positive or negative energies may be only as strong as your good or bad karmas done to this dog are. For example, if you harass the dog for some time, you may get a small amount of negative energy. If you beat it for some time, you may get more negative energy in response. If you injure it badly or kill it, you may have to deal with an even bigger amount of negative energy. Though you may only receive a small amount of negative energy by harassing an animal, even a small amount of negative energy added to your aura is going to make you more vulnerable to sufferings as your aura becomes more negative. Hence you are losing and not gaining.

Let's look at other entities like plants, rivers and other naturally occurring things. Let's see how these entities transfer energy. Suppose you have planted and raised an apple tree. Suppose you've worked hard on it and it has grown into a big fruit-bearing tree. Each time you served this tree with water, added fertilizer or tended to it in other ways, the tree receives positive energy from your side. In response to such energy, it releases positive energy which gets added to your aura, making it more positive.

However, it doesn't stop here and it goes further. Since it is a fruit-yielding tree, it starts bearing apples. These apples reach people and they eat them. Each time a person eats an apple from this tree, he is benefitted in terms of hunger, health, taste and other aspects. Accordingly, a corresponding amount of positive energy is sent by such person to the tree. This entire mechanism works on subconscious level in a way that such person may not even consciously realize that he has sent positive energy to the tree.

Hence this person may send positive energy to the aura of the tree which bore this apple. Like human beings; all animals, species and other phenomena in this universe carry unique auras. This is because aura is a collection of energies and each entity in the universe is made up of energies. Hence each one of these entities carries an aura.

As the positive energy of this person gets added to the aura of the tree, a similar response may be generated by the tree. It feels thankful to the person (you) who planted it and served it continuously. Through gratitude, positive energy is transferred from the tree to you. Accordingly, this energy is added to your aura. As people eat more and more apples from this tree, more and more positive energy flows to you. Hence you keep gaining positive energy.

It should be noted that a part of the positive energy sent to this tree by people eating the apples may be transferred through this tree to you, if you're letting people enjoy the fruits of this tree for free. However, if you own this apple tree, you sell its fruits and get money in return, you have already been rewarded. In this case, the positive energy from people eating apples may be added to the tree alone.

This is because you have already received your share of positive energy or rewards in form of money that was paid for apples. Hence you may not deserve more positive energy, as one can only get a specific amount of positive or negative energy in return for good or bad karmas that he does. If you claim instant rewards for something good you do, there may be little or no positive energy added to your aura. This is because you have already been paid for your good karmas in form of money or other good things.

Looking at some other facts, the person planting and serving a tree may be rewarded with positive energy or money or something else, only if he had charged nothing for planting such tree and for taking care of the tree. Suppose someone has a paid job of growing and managing a number of apple trees. He may not receive much positive energy when the fruits of these trees are eaten by people, as he already received money in return for his services. This means that his good karmas were already rewarded. Therefore, he may not deserve more positive energy or rewards for these karmas.

When you do bad things to others, they are hurt and accordingly, negative energies are released through their auras. These energies target you. At times, you may instantly get punished for such bad karmas whereas at times you may be able to skip the punishments. In such cases, negative energies are added to your aura, which may ensure that you don't skip such punishments forever. These energies may bring punishments to you, later on.

Suppose you engage in a fight with a comparatively weak person, when you don't have any just reason to do so. The other person may not be able to defend himself and/or cause you as much harm as you may cause him. Accordingly, a corresponding amount of negative energy may be released by him and it may get added to your aura. This energy may make your aura more negative, making sure that you are punished for this bad karma at a later time.

Looking at the same example from a different angle, suppose you get into a fight with a person equal in strength or a person stronger than you. Here again, there is no just reason for this fight and you may simply want to take your frustration out or prove a point. The other guy is fully capable of causing equal or more damage to you. Hence you may receive more physical damage than him. This is instant punishment for your bad karma. Since you have received due punishment on instant basis, the equation is settled and no negative energy may be added to your aura.

Hence if you do a good deed and get rewarded for it duly, you may not get positive energy added to your aura to be rewarded later. Similarly, if you do a bad karma and get punished for it duly, you may not get any negative energy added to your aura to be punished later. However, if you do a good deed and don't get rewarded instantly, or you only get rewarded partly, you may get due positive energy added to your aura. Such energy may bring pending rewards to you at a later time. Similarly, if you do a bad deed and you don't get punished for it instantly, or you get partial punishment for it, you may get due amount of negative energy added to your aura. This energy may bring the pending punishment to you at a later time.

It means anyone who is being paid for a job but he's not doing it properly, may be engaging in bad karmas. This is because he is given rewards in form of money; and he may not deserve them fully or partly; since he's not keeping his end of the bargain. Since he's being rewarded with more than he deserves, a negative balance becomes due. This adds negative energy to his aura.

Therefore, when you commit to deliver a certain amount of work for a certain reward, complete it or do your duty properly as otherwise, you may gather negative energy. Such energy may cause instant problems, which means that you may get fired from the job or your contract may be terminated. In case none of these things happen, negative energy may be added to your aura, as you have somehow managed to get the rewards and haven't done what you committed to do in return for such rewards.

On the other hand, if you are paid for a job and you are putting in equal amount of work or more amount of work than what you committed, you are justifying the rewards or you're doing more than that. If you're doing more; corresponding amount of positive energy may get added to your aura. This energy may bring you good results later on.

Looking at another important aspect of this theory; the amount of positive or negative energy added to your aura by various entities is dependent on their value in the system. Among all living beings like plants, animals and human beings; good or bad karmas done to plants or trees add the least amount of positive or negative energies to your aura. Good or bad karmas done to animals add comparatively stronger positive or negative energies to your aura. The strongest type of positive or negative energies are added to your aura when you do good or bad to human beings.

As a rule, more conscience a species may grow, more valuable it is. Trees can only work in some specific ways and even if they wish, they can't work in other ways. For example, a tree may not choose to provide shade to some people and not provide the same to some other people. Animals are also guided more by instincts and less by their conscious decisions. For example, a lion may feel helpless if he chooses to eat grass. Hence he may have no choice but to kill.

Humans are blessed with conscious choices almost in all situations. Hence a human can rise as high as God and he may drop as low as the devil. It means the potential to grow is maximum in humans, followed by animals and then followed by trees. Hence humans are valued the most in this system. Taking an example, thousands of trees can't produce a single human being. However, one human being can plant thousands of trees.

Likewise, hundreds of animals can't cater to a human in the way; a single human can cater to them. For instance, if a human falls ill or gets wounded, there is nothing much that animals may do. On the other hand, a single human being can treat the wounds of many animals. Hence humans are valued the most and good or bad done to them results in the highest amounts of reciprocal positive or negative energies.

This is how the concept of transfer of positive or negative energy in response to positive or negative karmas works. Though there may be many other aspects of this concept as this is a vast subject; we've covered the basics.

Addition of Energy through People and Places

People whose company you seek and places you visit can add energy to your aura. Hence they may influence your aura positively or negatively.

Though such influences may not bring direct profits or losses to you; without you engaging in good or bad karmas, such influences are capable of motivating or convincing your mind to do good or bad karmas. Accordingly, you are likely to be rewarded or punished. Hence people and places you visit are also important for the equation of energy.

Almost all species and other entities in the universe carry unique equations of energy in the form of auras. Most places initially may not carry strong auras of their own and the positivity or negativity they carry is supplied by the type of positive or negative people visiting and staying at these places. Once a place has sufficient energy, it may then receive energy as well as transfer energy.

Hence our houses, offices, entertainment venues, religious places, pubs, bars, hotels, hospitals, jails and other places including even our cars and other vehicles have their own auras. Such auras may have been initially supplied by us to them and these auras keep changing based on their interactions with various entities.

Have you wondered why you feel at peace, and why you relax when you go to a religious place but you get strange and perhaps scary vibes when you visit a cemetery? Similarly the type of vibes or energy or aura that you get from a bar versus that from a religious place, may be quite different.

Starting with places; all places gather energy from human beings, other species and entities that visit or stay at these places. Accordingly, each place has an aura which keeps changing continuously, depending on how many species are visiting that place; or staying at that place. The definition of a place in context of energy-theory is a place that is bound by certain visible or invisible boundaries.

Apart from that, the aura of a place is influenced by the kind of positive or negative activities performed within the boundaries of such place. For this reason, you may have felt that the vibes of a place where good deeds are done on regular basis are different from the vibes of a place where activities taking place are not good. The influences of positive or negative activities done at a place are much higher than the influences of people visiting or staying at such place, in most cases. This is because activities add more energy to the aura of a place in comparison to people who visit or stay at the same place.

Therefore in terms of energy and aura, your house or apartment is one place, whereas your neighbor's house is different, though it may be an adjoining apartment. This is why even two adjoining places like two apartments can have two different energy equations, as different types of people may be living there and different types of activities may be conducted there.

Let's see how this transfer works. Taking a religious place as an example, activities performed at such place include regular prayers, preaching, sharing good thoughts and serving others. Since all these activities release positive energy, such religious place is continuously supplied with positive energy. Accordingly, the positivity of this place increases. Hence such places may have strong positive auras.

Apart from that, most people staying at or visiting religious places may do more good karmas than bad ones. Hence their auras may be more positive than negative. It means they may add more positive energy than negative. In general, people with highly negative auras don't visit religious places as much as people with positive auras do. As a result, the amount of negative energy added to these places may be much lower in comparison to that of positive energy.

Since these places carry highly positive auras, parts of this energy may be transferred to people visiting such places. Accordingly, you may gain positive energy when you visit religious places.

You may have heard that some specific religious places carry more importance than other ones; especially the places where some saints, incarnations of gods or other likewise souls stayed for long periods of time. The auras of such people are positive as well as extremely strong. There may not be even traces of negativity in their auras. At the same time; their auras may be so strong that the effects cast by them may sustain for hundreds or thousands of years. Stronger is an aura; stronger and more lasting are the effects cast by it.

Such people have stayed at such places and they have engaged in practices like mediation at such places. Such practices generate extremely high amount of positive energy.

Such energy may still be present at these places; since such strong energy may easily last for hundreds or thousands of years; though it may get weaker with time. Hence when you visit one such place, you may attract a lot of positive energy from it.

It should be noted that not everyone may receive the same amount of positive energy from a religious/positive place. Though one such place may try to transfer the same amount to everyone, each may respond differently.

This is because different people have different strengths of receiving positive and negative energies, depending on the natures and strengths of their auras. A person with strong positive aura may attract a lot of positive energy from one such place, since positive energy attracts positive energy and it repels negative energy. A person with relatively weak positive aura may attract less amount of positive energy from one such place; depending on the strength of his aura.

A person with weak negative aura may attract even less amount of positive energy, since he has an even weaker tendency to welcome positive energy. This is because his aura is primarily negative and such aura tends to attract more negative energy than positive energy.

A person with highly negative aura may not attract much energy from one such religious place. Negative energy attracts the same and it repels positive energy. It is like darkness and light don't stay at the same place. There's either darkness or light. Hence they are naturally opposed to each other. Therefore, the aura of one such person may strongly repel positive energy radiating from a highly positive place like religious place.

As a result, he may start feeling uncomfortable at one such place. Hence he may not stay there for long and he may not visit such place often. For this reason, people with highly negative auras may not visit or stay at places with highly positive auras. Hence religious places may not witness much negative energy transferred to them through people.

Places with negative auras like slaughter houses, mental asylums, cemeteries, casinos and other such places may add negative energies to people who visit them. Here also, different people may attract different amounts of negative energy; depending on the natures and strengths of their auras. People with highly negative auras may attract maximum energy from such places, followed by people with relatively weaker negative auras.

People with slightly positive auras may attract even less negative energy and people with positive auras having significant strengths may attract even less. People with strong positive auras may not attract much negative energy from such places, since their auras may repel such energy. Such people may keep their auras intact, even if they visit such negative places.

It means that people with strong negative auras may not benefit much by visiting positive places alone. Hence they need to engage in good karmas in order to receive positive energy. As more and more positive energy is added to their auras, such auras become less negative. This helps them attract more positive energy from positive places.

This brings us to an important point that extreme types of auras are the most difficult to change into the opposite type. Strong positive auras may repel negative energy whereas strong negative auras may repel positive energy.

Hence much more effort may be needed in order to change a strong negative aura into a positive one. The same holds for a strong positive aura also.

Let's try to understand this theory from the angle of the conscious and subconscious mind. As negativity in the aura of a person goes high, it starts resisting positive energy coming from positive places and positive people. This is because through his conscious mind and conscious efforts, this person has instructed his subconscious to attract more and more negative energy. The subconscious registers this pattern. Hence it starts attracting more negative energy and it starts repelling positive energy. This way, more and more negative energy may be added to his aura and little positive energy may be added.

Apart from that, his negative subconscious may encourage him to engage more and more in bad karmas. Such karmas may add even more negative energy to his subconscious/aura. As a result, the equation may keep deteriorating with time and he may possess more and more negative energy. It means his negative subconscious attracts more negative energy through people, places and karmas. As it becomes more negative, it attracts even more negative energy and this process goes on; until this person is fed up and he starts engaging in positive conscious efforts.

However, such efforts may require a lot of will power and resistance. This is because the subconscious may stand in opposition to the conscious. The conscious wants positivity but the subconscious has a strong script for negativity. Hence there is a direct clash between the conscious and the subconscious. Since the latter is much stronger than the former; it may be a hard battle for the former to fight and win.

Despite all that; it is the conscious mind alone which can win this battle. With time and effort, the conscious may rewrite the script/pattern on the subconscious and the subconscious may start executing the new script.

On the other hand, a strongly positive subconscious/aura attracts a lot of positivity from people and places. At the same time, it encourages you to engage in more and more positive karmas as well as have more and more positive attitude. This way, you keep adding more and more positive energy to your aura. As it becomes more positive, it attracts even more positivity and it repels negativity with even more strength. Hence you may become more and more positive with time; unless conscious efforts are done to rewrite the script written on the subconscious. Here also, it may take long time and much effort to change your highly positive subconscious/aura into a negative one.

Have you ever wondered why saints and enlightened people don't seem to put in much conscious effort to engage in more and more good/neutral karmas? It seems like engaging in good karmas comes naturally to them. Whenever something comes naturally to you; it means it comes from your subconscious. Their subconscious minds have become highly positive. Such subconscious minds keep executing scripts written on them all the time; where such scripts tend to attract more and more positive energy. Hence they effortlessly engage in good/neutral karmas.

Such stage of having a highly positive subconscious/aura is very difficult to achieve. However, once it is achieved, there may be no turning back, since your aura may become so positive that it may not let any negative energy build up or come in.

It means once you start adding positive energy to your aura; such positive energy helps you attract more positive energy and this goes on. Likewise, once you start adding negative energy to your aura; such negative energy encourages you to add more negative energy and this too goes on. Hence choose wisely which type of energy you wish to add to your aura.

Let's see how energy is added through people. The theory of transfer is similar. People with positive auras tend to add positive energy to your aura whereas people with negative auras tend to add negative energy to your aura. Here again, you may receive different amounts of positive or negative energy; depending on how strongly positive or negative your aura is.

When two or more people meet, their auras try to influence one another. Suppose you have a meeting with a person and you spend about 30 minutes with him. During these 30 minutes, both of you may try to influence the other; through your auras as well as through conscious and subconscious efforts. Depending on the type and strengths of your auras; different outcomes are possible.

Suppose both of you have positive auras and your aura is stronger than his. In this case, he'll be influenced more by you than you may be influenced by him. If his aura is stronger than yours; you may be influenced more by him than he may be influenced by you. If you have a positive aura and he has a negative aura; the equation depends on the strength of your auras. If his aura is mildly negative and your aura is strongly positive, you may be able to influence him after some effort. However, if his aura is strongly negative; you two may not click. There may be strong repulsion between you two.

Weak positive and negative auras are most vulnerable to changes. This is the why some people though good in nature may end up doing bad things, when convinced or provoked by others with negative auras. Since their auras are weak; such auras may be overpowered by those of negative people.

Hence they may end up engaging in bad karmas; despite being good people. This is why you should keep good company as good people may influence you to do good karmas; which may add positive energy to your aura. Company of bad people may on the other hand, end up making your aura more negative. Hence choose your company wisely.

THREE FACTORS ESSENTIAL FOR SUCCESS

As you collect positive energy through good karmas, people and places; such energy makes your aura more positive. This energy starts working to bring rewards for you.

Such energy starts making changes to your personality, in order to make you more capable of achieving certain specific goals that you wish to achieve. Your subconscious has a list of all your desires and resolutions. Your subconscious/aura tries to fulfil these desires with increased positive energies. Which desires may be fulfilled first, depends on some factors.

The first factor is the strength of a specific desire. Stronger a desire is, more priority your subconscious attaches to it. Hence the subconscious tries to fulfil that desire first; which is on top of priority list. However, other factors may not allow it to do so at times. Looking at the next factor; the amount of karmic rewards or positive energy required for each desire is the next factor. Other factors may include your age, circumstances, gender and other relevant details.

Let's take an example to understand this concept in a better manner. Suppose you have a credit card and you earn reward points each time you use it. Such rewards points may be used to collect rewards of your liking, from a catalogue of rewards that the credit card company may have. Suppose you want a luxury watch as your reward and it needs 50,000 reward points. The first factor is your desire to get such luxury watch whereas the second factor is the number of points required to do so.

Hence you may have desire but you may not have sufficient points. Suppose you have 40,000 points at a time. It means you still can't get this watch though it is on top of your priority list among the items in the catalogue. This leaves you with two options. You can choose to wait till you earn the required number of rewards or you can choose to settle for something else which you can get with 40,000 reward points.

One aspect of the subconscious works like this. The subconscious keeps assessing the desires as well as the energy required to achieve them. Hence a desire may be on top of your priority list but it may still not be fulfilled, if you don't have sufficient positive energy to fulfil it. If you have sufficient energy as well as desire; such wish may be fulfilled.

Looking at other factors; suppose your strongest desire is to achieve great success as an actor. Three major factors affect fulfilment of this desire. The first one is the desire itself. It means you have to have a desire first; in order for it to be fulfilled. The second factor is the required amount of effort. It means you need to learn how to act and do all other things which are required to achieve success as an actor. The third factor is luck factor which means the amount of positive energy required to fulfill this desire.

Suppose you have the desire and you keep making conscious efforts to achieve success as an actor. As you gain more and more positive energy through various media; your aura/subconscious may become stronger.

Hence your subconscious may make many good changes to your personality whereas your aura may attract more opportunities. As a result, you may start witnessing success. As you achieve more and more positive energy; the quantum of such success may also increase.

Suppose you become a good or very good actor but not a great actor like you desire; by the time you die. This unfulfilled desire is dealt with on priority basis and you may become an actor in the next life also. In this life, you may achieve even more success; depending on the three essential factors. This trend may continue life after life until you have accumulated sufficient positive energy to completely fulfil your desire. You may fulfil your desire, it may get deleted from the list and the next desire may take its place.

This trend may go on and on for hundreds or thousands of lives, with new desires taking places of the ones which have been fulfilled. During a particular life; you may develop spiritual tendencies and you may witness reduction in desires. It means you may not create as many desires now as you used to. As the number of new desires drops and the old ones keep getting fulfilled where some of them may be dropped; you start having less number of desires. You may drop a desire if you wish, since it is your desire.

This trend may continue for many lives and a moment may come when you may not have any unfulfilled desire; and you may not create new conscious desires. This is the state of liberation where you're free from conscious desires and the wish of the universal conscience is your wish now. It means you're comfortable with whatever happens to you. You don't wish to make changes to anything and you don't judge anything or anyone.

Looking at some other factors; suppose apart from being a great actor, you desire to enjoy attention as well as company of a lot of women. At the beginning of a particular life, you may not have sufficient energy to fulfill this desire; even to a significant extent. Hence you may not be blessed with the kind of physique or looks which attract a lot of females. With time, efforts and more positive energy; you may start achieving success as an actor. Suppose you achieve good amount of success by the time you turn 60.

Since you don't have an attractive physique and you've reached an age which may not support the kind of physical pleasures with women that you may be looking for; this desire may be postponed to the next life; even though you have sufficient energy to fulfil it. Your body has limits and your subconscious knows these limits. Hence it may give you a fair chance in the next life where you may enjoy success as an actor as well as company of women from young age. Likewise, there are other situational factors which may hinder fulfilment of a particular desire. However, the three most important factors are the desire element, the effort and energy required.

This system works well as long as the object of your desire is a thing or an abstract phenomenon. When it comes to people, the system works in a different way. This is because things and abstract phenomena don't have wishes of their own. It means a luxury car doesn't have a wish as to who should buy it. Whosoever spends money, the car belongs to him. Likewise, stardom doesn't have a choice of its own and whoever fits the criteria may achieve it.

When it comes to people, it's different. This is because people have freewill. Due to such freewill, the third factor which is the amount of positive energy required may not work here. Hence you may become the richest, the most powerful or the most desirable man in the world; but the woman you desire the most may still not be interested in you. On the other hand, you may have average type of success and resources but the woman you desire the most may still love you.

When it comes to people; three essential factors change. They are; the desire element, the effort and mutual equation of auras. It means if you like a woman, you engage in efforts to get into a relationship with her. If your aura is strongly in accordance with her aura, you desire may be fulfilled. If you two have different types of auras; she may not take interest in you or she may reject you.

If that happens; this desire may remain unfulfilled. If you're not willing to drop this desire and the woman is not willing to take interest in you; all your positive energy can't help you in this case. However, your subconscious may still help you. It creates a demand in the system of nature and as a result of such demand; you may be born again during the same timelines as those of such woman.

Your subconscious may bring you closer to this woman in the next life; and you may try all over again. If the woman takes interest in you; your desire may be fulfilled as well as deleted. If she doesn't show interest; the equation may be postponed to the next life. This may continue for as many lives as it takes; until one of the two things happen. Either the woman engages in a relationship with you or you drop this desire. When one of these things happen; you may get rid of such desire. For this reason; desires for people may be much more difficult to fulfil compared to desires for things and abstract phenomena.

To summarize; three essential factors required to fulfill desires related to things and abstract phenomena are; the desire element, the effort and energy required. When it comes to fulfil desires related to people, three essential factors are; the desire element, the effort and mutual equation of auras.

Section 2

How to Improve yourself

Identify Your Problem First

In order to gain more positive energy, you should engage in more positive karmas. Doing so is essential but it may not be sufficient. There are other factors which are important and some of them may become more important if you don't wish to achieve any type of good results and you want to achieve specific good results.

The first thing to understand is that each individual is unique. Likewise, their issues may be different from other individuals. At times, various people may seem to suffer from similar problems, but the causes may be different. For example, a headache may be caused because of low blood pressure, high blood pressure, hangover, hunger, lack of sleep, stress and many other reasons. Though the end result is the same which is headache, the causes may be different in different cases. Depending on the causes, different treatments may be required to relieve various people suffering from headache.

Hence, stop looking for general solutions and try to find out what works for you. It is interesting to see that you choose a specific cream that suits your skin type, a specific soap, specific types of clothes as well as shoes; and all other specific types of things. You may even choose specific types of people who go well with you. Isn't it good that you choose specific guidelines also, which work well to improve your personality; instead of trying anything and everything in general.

In order to treat a problem, you first need to identify it. If you are not successful in profession, relationships, education and/or other spheres of your life, after all your desires and efforts; it means your aura has specific types of negative energies which put limits on good results. In order to improve your chances; you'll first need to identify these energies. Since energies form patterns and patterns mean habits, you're supposed to look for specific habits.

Through good karmas, you need to gain sufficient positive energy. At the same time, through desires and efforts, you need to develop specific patterns which may help you achieve specific results.

Auras of most people contain mixtures of various types of positive and negative energies. Various types of positive energies may bless you with various types of good habits whereas various types of negative energies may trouble you with bad habits. We've already discussed that the subconscious is a creature of habit. Hence various patterns/scripts formed by various energies on your subconscious reflect in form of habits.

Specific types of negative energies create specific types of bad habits, tastes and flaws in us and we may suffer due to them. Since different people may have different types of negative energies, the reasons for their failures may be different, though the end results may be the same.

Hence you need to fix specific energies which cause specific habits; and the first step is to identify them. Such identification may be done, broadly in two ways. If you're an aware type of person; you may look into yourself and find out what your flaws or bad habits are. If you're not that aware; take help from people who are closest to you, since they may know you better than you. Ask them to tell you about your flaws and they may enlist most of them.

Once you've identified your problems, the next step is to deal with them. While trying to fix your problems; always keep in mind not to follow general guidelines. At times, they may not work for you and at times; they may hurt you. Taking an example, suppose you suffer from the problem of arguing too much. Hence you may face problems in profession and especially in relationships. Though general guidelines for improvement may advise you to learn more, be more informed and gain more confidence through such knowledge; such practices may aggravate this problem.

This is because you already have a habit of engaging in arguments; and more knowledge may add fuel to the fire. Hence you may end up having more and longer arguments which may cause even more problems for you. It means you need a different approach to fix this problem. Hence you need to learn to reduce this habit and at the same time; you need to make sure that you don't supply yourself with more and more unnecessary information about various topics; at least till your problem is sorted.

Learning is a good habit but it may cause problems in some cases. More you learn; better you may be at presenting yourself and convincing other people. This is good in general. However, if you have a habit of arguing too much; learning more and more may aggravate this problem, as you may have more facts to support your arguments. Hence you should choose selective learning until this problem is sorted. It means you should learn what is required for your job and other important spheres and stay away from the rest. We'll deal with this topic in more details, in the relevant chapter.

To summarize, you need to specifically identify your problems and then engage in specific measures to fix them. When you do that, you may witness improvement in many spheres of life.

Too Much Copying

The first habit that you should learn to improve is that of blindly copying others. Each individual is unique and what works for others may not work for you. On the contrary, it may cause problems for you.

Hence don't copy anyone blindly and if you must copy someone, learn first why that habit works for him. If you are holding the same ground, it may work for you also. Taking an example, if you add blue to a colourless solution, the solution may turn blue. However, if you add blue to a yellow solution, it may turn green. Similarly you may get a variety of different colours if you add blue to solutions of different colours. Though you add the same colour to different solutions, the resultant colour is different in all cases, depending on the original colour of solution.

Blue here signifies a habit that makes a person successful. Since you want to be blue, you add that colour or that habit to yourself by copying that habit, not being aware about your original colour which means personality type. Hence you may witness benefit or you may come across problems; depending on your overall personality.

Considering another example, suppose an actor spends 2 hours at gym every day and he quotes that his muscular body is the key to his success. If you try to copy this habit without looking at your personality type and circumstances; you may end up paying more than you get. It means your financial status, dietary habits, work routines and/or your personality type may not support spending this much money or time on building muscle. Hence you may not benefit much from this practice and instead; you may face problems.

Taking another example, suppose a person with very fair skin is tanning in the sun so that he may achieve tanned look. Is it wise for a person with dark or very dark skin to copy him and start tanning? The fair person is trying to tan in order to achieve a better look by adding darker touch to his complexion. The other person is already having a lot of dark colour added to his skin. Hence he may only end up looking even darker, which may spoil his look.

The key point here is balance. The fair person is trying to achieve balance by making his skin somewhat darker so that he may fall in the middle range. If you must copy him; you need to copy his intention and not his outward expression. It means you may also try to balance the colour of your skin. However in order to do that; you need to find ways to make it fairer and not those which make it darker. If you do that; you may be doing the opposite of what he's doing in terms of outward expression. However, you're doing the same in deeper sense, since you're both trying to reach the middle range for your skin colour.

Considering another example, suppose someone is on a restricted diet as he wishes to loose extra fat. You on the other hand may not have even healthy amount of fat in your body, which means you may be skinny. Hence it is not wise to follow this person and cut your calories, even if he's your favourite celebrity. If you wish to copy him; copy in essence. He's trying to bring his body fat levels within normal ranges. Since his fat levels are in the higher range, he's trying to reduce them. You on the other hand are in the lower range. Hence you should try to add some pounds so that you may also fall in normal range.

It is like if four people are running towards a common destination from four different directions; they are trying to achieve the same thing but their outward expressions may look different. One way of looking at it is that all of them are running in different directions which may even be opposite ones like one of them is running east and another one is running west. However in the deepest sense; they are running for the same objective. It means each one of them can achieve such objective by running in different direction and not in the same direction.

Hence don't start running east by copying someone. You may already be far east from your objective. Hence you need to run west in order to achieve the same objective. Running east may take you further away from the objective. Likewise, you may need to run north if you are far south from the objective.

Assess your situation first and then decide what should be done from there; instead of copying people who may be in altogether different situations.

Laziness

Laziness is one negative habit which can take away all the good things from you. It goes against the basic law of success which says that in order to achieve success, you need three things; strong desire, effort and luck or positive energy. With laziness, the factor of effort goes away directly whereas the other two factors are weakened indirectly.

Laziness lies in direct opposition to effort. Lazier you are, less effort you put in and accordingly, less are the chances of success. Without effort, it is difficult to achieve anything in life. All your positive energy can only ensure that if you try a thing, you may succeed. However, you have to try first. As laziness increases, you tend to try less, thereby reducing your chances to achieve success.

Even the ones who are blessed with luck factor have to engage in continuous efforts in order to make the most of their positive energy. For example, a champion player may not remain a champion if he becomes lazy and starts performing poorly. Though luck may help him when he needs it, luck can't play for him and he has to do so by himself. Likewise, all other successful people also have to engage in efforts in order to achieve and maintain success. Without effort, they may not even be successful despite all the luck they may have.

Looking at the other two essential factors needed for success, laziness affects the desire factor. As laziness increases, you may stop developing strong desires for various things. Through laziness, your conscious writes a script on the subconscious that you're incapable of achieving anything significant since you're not willing to put in required effort. Accordingly, your subconscious mind may start preventing you from having strong desires also, as it knows that there is no point in having such desires when you can't put due effort to fulfill them.

The next important factor required for success is luck or positive energy; and it is also affected by laziness. A lazy person engages in fewer karmas, whether good or bad, as he doesn't want to do much of anything. Accordingly, the amount of positive energy that he can add to his aura through good karmas decreases.

On the other hand, whatever positive energy he already has in his aura is continuously being spent by him to live his life. This is because even if he doesn't do much, he needs basic things like food and other things of daily need to survive. A part of his positive energy is spent each time he achieves one such thing. Hence the positivity of his aura may start decreasing and accordingly, his chances of achieving success decrease too.

Therefore, you simply can't afford the luxury of laziness as you may stop adding more positive energy to your aura and you may keep spending the already collected positive energy. If this keeps happening, your aura may become less and less positive at first and then; it may become more and more negative. Even if you live with the help of your parents or siblings, your aura passes on positive energy to them; each time they do something for you, which you should do instead. This way, you may run out of required positive energy at a point. This is when they may refuse to help you any longer.

Hence you need to start working on this problem at the earliest.

Let's see how this problem can be rectified. Through conscious acts of being lazy, your conscious mind has written a script on your subconscious. This script says you don't want to do much physical work. Accordingly, you subconscious starts discouraging you whenever you wish to engage in efforts because this is not who you are according to your subconscious.

In order to rectify this problem, you need to send repeated conscious messages to your subconscious; that you wish to engage in more and more efforts. With time and efforts, you may rewrite the script and your problem may go away.

Let's look at some important points which may help in rectifying this problem. Don't try to take big steps in the beginning and take small steps. Big things require a lot from your side and you may not have much due to being lazy. Though you may have the enthusiasm, your body and subconscious are working against you; since they are not accustomed to such efforts from you side. Hence you may witness physical as well as mental discomfort of high quantum. Such discomfort may not let you continue and you may end up discontinuing.

The subconscious can play various types of tricks on you due to which you may hear voices from inside. Such voices may try to discourage you or distract you. Some of them may go like, "this activity is not going to help much", "you're not capable of doing it, hence don't try" and "you should quit this activity and try another one which is more productive".

The last one is especially tricky since it is trying to distract you. It says though you're capable, the activity you chose is not right for you. Hence it may make you quit. Once you find a new activity, it may do the same and this may continue. Your subconscious may not let you engage in anything big since it stands in opposition to big efforts.

Basically, it stands in opposition to all types of efforts, whether small or big; due to the script you wrote on it. The subconscious poses resistance to all the things which go against the script written on it. As a rule, smaller are the changes, less is the resistance whereas bigger changes attract strong resistance. Since you're trying to achieve big things in the beginning, the subconscious may oppose you with great strength and you may not succeed because the subconscious is much stronger than the conscious.

Hence you should not use force to win over your subconscious and you should use tricks. Despite all the power that your subconscious has; the source of such power is your conscious mind. It means your conscious wrote a specific script on your subconscious and only your conscious can change this script. Hence you have two jobs at hand. The first one is to change the script and the second one is not to fight hard with your subconscious, while you're in the process of changing it. It means you need skill and patience to change the script of being lazy; and aggression alone is a bad idea.

People who want to be educated start from the first class and then they move ahead. Likewise, on your first day at a gym, you only try light exercises and you don't lift heavy weights. With time, your body may learn to do heavy lifting also. A baby learns to sit first, then it tries to stand, then walk and then run; where running may take years. It means you should start slow and then build up from there.

Therefore, start treating your laziness with the help of small activities. There are two advantages in doing so. The first one is that in order to engage in small activities, you don't need much effort. The second one is that through these small but conscious activities, your conscious mind starts sending more and more signals to your subconscious mind. These signals say that you are not lazy and you like to work. Since the activities are small ones; your subconscious may not pose strong resistance to them. As a result, you may get through.

With time and effort, your subconscious may start posing less resistance and it may then start encouraging you. Once that happens; you should increase the quantum of your efforts. Once your subconscious has adjusted to this level also; you should further increase the intensity. This way, you can build up efforts and rewrite the script on your subconscious, slowly but surely.

Another advantage in doing so is that your body may also have sufficient time to accommodate itself to the changes in your working routines. Since you're building up gradually, your body may also have no problems in making adjustments.

It is like a video game where the first level is easy and it makes you think that you can play. The next level is comparatively difficult but by the time you reach there, you're able to adjust since the change is gradual. This way, you keep playing and in a matter of days; you may be able to attempt difficult or very difficult levels.

Imagine what may happen if a game features the most difficult level as its first round? Most people who try such game may not like it as it may be too difficult for them and they may quit it. Hence start with small things and then build up; instead of going for the last round first.

Let's discuss some day to day activities which are small but which can effectively treat laziness. Some common favourite things for most lazy people are to sit on a chair or sofa; and relax on a sofa or couch while lying. Hence we need to start from here. If lazy people can start moving more and more from these two positions; they may see good results.

In the beginning, simply make a plan that whenever you are sitting or lying except when you are sleeping, you will get up once every 5 or 10 minutes and you will move. You may do so to get a glass of water, to see if the door is locked, to check if the gas stove is turned off or simply to take a round of your house or the place you are at.

It may sound like a small activity but it does its job. Each time you get up and take a round, this conscious activity sends a message to your subconscious mind that you are not lazy anymore and you can get up, move and do anything; anytime you want. This is when you start erasing the old script on your subconscious mind and start writing a new one.

As you master this act of getting up and moving around, in a matter of weeks or even in days, you may start getting feelings or inner voices which may stop you from sitting idle or lying idle. This means that the new script has started taking place of the old script. Accordingly, your subconscious mind may start sending encouraging inner voices to you.

The essence of these voices may be that if you're supposed to get up every 10 minutes; what is the point of lying in the first place, and why not do something instead? It means your subconscious is encouraging you to quit lying and start engaging in various types of jobs. If you choose to ignore these voices, your subconscious may start making you feel uncomfortable when you try to sit or lie. When that happens; you're ready for the next level.

At the next level, choose something which is somewhat more difficult but which is not a lot more difficult than your first task. For instance, you may start engaging in small household chores and spend more and more time in them. One such good practice is that you should take the job of going to the nearby market and get the items of daily need. If you have an option, you should pick a shop or store which is at a walking distance from your house. You should split this job in a way that you visit such store; two, three or four times a day.

As you start moving more and as you start doing more, your body will get accustomed to increased levels of physical performance. Accordingly, laziness decreases. At the same time, your subconscious mind is getting more messages that you like to work. With time and effort, you may get through this level also; and the script on your subconscious may change more in your favour. Once you master the activities in this level, your subconscious mind may start motivating you for the next level; again through the inner voices. It means you're ready for the next level.

In the third step, start doing more things at work. Start spending more time with your girlfriend or wife and do more to help her out. Start engaging in physical activities like brisk walking, running or any other such activity. Start learning something valuable and start developing a skill or start polishing a skill if you already have one. Engage in whichever one of the above mentioned spheres is the one that you like the most; and you may see significant progress in that sphere. Remember, for the same effort you put in, in different spheres of life, your gains will be the maximum in the sphere that you like the most.

The reason for such gains is simple. When you have a strong desire to do something, you are more likely to succeed in it since strong desire is one of the three essential factors required for success. Hence it is always helpful if you can get your efforts supported by a strong desire. This way, you will have two out of three required factors working in your favour. Accordingly, your chances of success are better. Hence when you reach this level and are ready to work on a practical sphere of your life, don't just randomly choose any sphere and start with the sphere that you like the most.

Now you have an idea about what types of activities should be there in each level. Based on your choices and circumstances, you may choose different activities. The idea is to start slow and build up gradually. Don't try to jump any level until you start feeling positively uncomfortable which means the level becomes so easy that you wish to play a harder one. Until that happens; keep playing on the same level. During this practice, speed may be your enemy and patience as well as perseverance may be your best friend.

Leaving Things Incomplete

The habit of leaving things incomplete is a specific type of laziness and that is why we are dealing with it right after laziness. This habit may also be called careless attitude.

There are people who may not be called duly lazy, though they display specific types of laziness. One among them is leaving things incomplete. Such people may do only as much as is required to say that they've done a job. However, they almost always miss the finishing touch. They are happy doing the core parts of most jobs and they don't care for polishing and furnishing. For example, one such person may complete about 80% of a project and then let it hang for a long period of time. Looking at other variations; he may complete the project in time but he may not present it in time or he may not present it in an organized manner, though the project may be good.

Looking at other examples, some of these people may cook delicious food but they may not serve it properly and they may lack finishing touch. Some others may set 2 Km run on treadmills and then stop at 1.5 or 1.6 Km or they may get off the machines when the calorie reading is 260 or 360, instead of completing 300 or 400. Some of them may decide to climb mountains but they may return from 60-70% of the way. Some others may have beautiful houses but they may not maintain them well.

Hence things may be found lying here and there, instead of being at their proper places. They may have good clothes and shoes but they may not care much about their cleanliness and conditions. They may leave some of their food items uneaten. They may often forget to carry some important things while leaving homes, like their driving licenses.

Most such people may throw their clothes here and there when they come home; instead of putting them at their proper places. Such items may keep lying here and there for some hours or even for a day or two; before they pick them up. Likewise, they may throw their shows and they may pick them up when they need them the next time.

Looking into their bathrooms; many such clothing items may be found hanging there, which have no use in bathroom. There may be some old toothbrushes, some bottles of shampoo and other such products which are old or very old. Such items may be waiting to be thrown to the bin for many months or even for years.

Looking into their kitchens, many grocery items may not be categorized and/or named properly and some of them may be found in wrong sections. Unwashed dishes may be there in sinks at such times of the day when they should not be. Some items of partly eaten food may be still lying in the kitchens; waiting to be refrigerated or thrown to the bins. Their houses may not be managed properly. Their car keys may be at wrong places, TV remotes and other remotes may be lying here and there; and they may often forget where they put their cell phones and other such items.

Such people suffer from a specific type of laziness. Due to this negative trait, they may not be dependable and that may hurt their chances of success in most spheres of life. This habit can do much damage in profession as well as relationship; as the other parties may get tired of such attitude of these people.

As one such person begins to leave things incomplete; he sends conscious signals to his subconscious mind that he likes things this way. With time and repeated acts; the subconscious may register it as a script and it may start executing it. When that happens; his subconscious may start encouraging him to do so more and more. Hence he may start hearing inner voices. Some of these voices may be like, "it's all right to leave clothes on sofa for a while and there nothing wrong with it", "you can wash the dishes later and there's no hurry", "it's just a remote and you can put it anywhere" and many other such voices. Such voices may encourage him to leave one aspect or another of most things incomplete.

With time, this habit may grow stronger. When that happens, it may start affecting the spheres which may be important or very important like profession, relationships and health. Taking an example, if one such person is a tailor and he is stitching a suit for you, he may not deliver it in time. He may present an excuse that the suit is almost finished and only buttons and/or zips need to be done. Hence he may ask you to visit tomorrow or later. This may happen to most of his clients. With time; he may build up a reputation of being untrustworthy; and it may hurt his professional growth.

Likewise, if one such person is a car mechanic and he's promised you to deliver your car by 5 in the evening; he may make excuses when you visit him at that time. He may tell you that the washing part or some other part is left and you should come back after some time. If one such person is a teacher, his students may complain that he skips one thing or another from every chapter. Though he may be good at teaching, he may almost always deliver less than 100%.

Likewise, such people may not bother about getting regular health checkups. Even if they find something is wrong with them; they may postpone as long as they can, before visiting doctors. Such practice may at times land them into serious health issues. After they visit doctors; they may not follow up properly and some of them may not follow up at all. They may not take their medicines regularly and they may often skip doses.

Looking at relationships; such people may often show up late for their dates and/or they may not arrange movie tickets till last moments though they may have made such plans many days ago. Likewise, they may not deposit their kids' fees before deadlines and some of them may often pay such fees after the deadlines; with fines. When they go to markets to purchase items of daily need; they may often skip or forget some items and they may almost never purchase everything on the lists they may have. Likewise, they may deliver less than 100% in most other spheres of their lives.

All these people may be perfectly capable of delivering 100%, but they may simply not be interested due to the subconscious script of leaving things incomplete. This can make them less dependable at times and completely undependable at times.

Let's see how this habit should be handled. Going with the basic rule, start with small changes and then build up. In most cases; you only need to put conscious efforts for changing small things and the big ones may change with time, if you've accomplished the first task. This is because almost everything big is made up of smaller units. If you change the units; the bigger picture is changed.

When you start with small things, your subconscious may not pose strong opposition. Hence it may be easy to do them, compared to big ones; as already discussed in the chapter named 'Laziness'. To start with, each time you get back home, make sure you put your clothes, shoes, watch and other such items at their proper places before you take rest or do something else, like eating a meal. Change first, put things at their proper places and then do something else. These are small things but they can bring big changes.

Through these acts, you start sending signals to your subconscious that doing things in proper manner is important for you. With time, your subconscious may register such messages and this level may become easy for you. In the next level, make sure you put your car keys, TV remote as well as other remotes, your cell phone and other such items at proper places chosen by you. This way; you'll always know where to find them when you need them. Since cell phone is a moving item; you may choose specific places for it in each room.

With time and effort, your subconscious may become fine with this level also. Hence you may not face problems while doing these things. When you reach such stage; your subconscious may encourage you to do more. It means you're ready for the next level.

Start applying these changes to bigger spheres of your life like profession, relationships and health. You may find that you're able to take most such things to completion, with effort and without strong resistance from your subconscious. This is because the subconscious has already replaced a part of the old script and it is in the process of replacing the rest.

Here also, don't do too much too soon. Start with small things and then build up gradually.

Bad Physical Shape

Bad physical shape means that you are too thin or are too fat. Though none of these conditions may devoid you of success, they can pose difficulties for you while reaching success or they can limit the amount of success you achieve.

For instance, this aspect may prove bad when you try to find a life partner of your choice. This is because in the present times; majority of people may be fitness conscious. Hence physical looks matter in this time and age, than they ever mattered before; at least during the beginning stages of such relationships. Since the beginning stage is a difficult one, being out of shape may hurt you more than you may imagine.

Suppose you have a number of positive traits in your personality and you're a good or very good person. However, you're out of shape; say you have 30-40 extra pounds on your body. This may block many women from being attracted to you since they may not like to date someone who has this much extra fat. Though you may be good or very good company, that may only come into play if you're given chances. Hence you may get rejected by many women on the basis of looks alone, though many of them may fall for you if they interact with you.

Hence keep your body in shape. Try not to have much extra fat on your body and try not to be too thin. Middle range is good for most things and it may be good here also.

Though building a physique may help you gain extra points for looks; falling in middle range may be sufficient in most cases.

Apart from that, being out of shape comes with a number of other disadvantages; especially if you're fatter or much fatter than an average person. The extra fat may take a toll on your physical performance in various spheres of life. Apart from that, it may make you vulnerable to a number of health issues. Hence keep your body in shape as that helps a lot.

Being physically fit doesn't necessarily mean you have to regularly go to a gym, lift heavy weights and start looking like the Hulk; as such routines can be difficult to follow on regular basis. This is because these routines involve costs and resources like gym fee, fuel expenses, special diets, time and other things.

Being physically fit simply means two things: the first one is that you should be in good physical shape. The second one is that you should be able to perform physical tasks. Hence you should engage in such activities which demand a good amount of physical strength or stamina like brisk walk or running, three to four times a week. Through these activities, your body may always be ready to perform. Through such conscious physical activities, you keep telling your subconscious mind that you need strength and stamina to perform. Accordingly, such strength and stamina is reserved for you and sooner than you know, such strength and stamina may become your best friend, as long as you keep performing your physical activities.

I am not against going to gym, lifting weights and building muscle. In fact, I love going to gym and building muscle. However, this book is not for me and it is for you.

Hence let's not discuss what works well for me and let's discuss what may work well for you. Going to gym may need fair amount of money, resources and time which not everyone may be able to afford. You may not have that much money or you may not afford that much time or extra diet.

It is not good to invite more problems in order to get rid of the one you have at hand. Hence you should take a balanced approach. If gym fits into your lifestyle and financial equation; you may go for it. If not, choose other options.

Building more muscle may have negative effect on some people who may be suffering from excessive aggression. Such people should stay away from building more muscle, as it may worsen their problem. Instead, they should find something else that suits them.

Brisk walking and running not only reduce unwanted fat from your body, but they also improve your physical strength, stamina and health. An added bonus is that walking and running are probably the most affordable exercises. Hence you don't have to pay anything to do them. The whole world is your gym and you can continue to walk and run without any problems or expenses. Whether it's a gym, park, road, mountain or sea shore, it doesn't matter as long as you exercise regularly to keep yourself in shape as well as to build and maintain strength and stamina.

Let's look at a helpful tip. When you start engaging in physical exercises, there will always be various physical activities which can give you the same or similar results. Such activities may include walking, brisk walking, jogging, running, cycling, skipping, swimming, aerobics and many other activities.

Try them one by one and you may find out that you are naturally good at some of them, just all right at some, and bad at some of them. Though you may think that you should improve yourself first in activities where you don't do well, this is exactly what you should not do. Instead, you should follow those activities more and more that you find most comfortable and convenient; with increased levels of resistance. This is because being comfortable while doing some specific physical activities means that you are naturally gifted there. It means you've done them a lot in your past lives.

You love the Sun for being bright and you love the Moon for being cool. Likewise, you may love various types of actors, singers, athletes, players and performers for what they are and you may not imagine changing them. It means you may not want your favourite player to quit sports and start acting. Likewise, you may not want your favourite actor to quit acting and start playing. This is because you know they're doing what they are best at doing.

Hence it's not a good idea to spend more and more time with cycling if you don't feel comfortable with it at all. While cycling, your mind may always be split in two; with one part telling you not to do it and the other part forcing you to take up this challenge. Your body may also support the part which says don't do it, since you may not cope very well with this exercise on physical level. Hence don't do it and find some other exercise.

Suppose, you feel very comfortable with running and you can sense that if you continue this activity, you can perform well or very well in a short period of time. Hence engage in it more and more, because you may be at your best, you may be able to burn more calories, increase strength and stamina. Apart from that, you love running and nothing can match a feeling of love or comfort.

Therefore, don't look pathetic and miserable while cycling where you get below average results. Instead, do more and more running where you dominate like a champion. There is a champion or winner within most of us. However, some of us are able to bring out that champion and many of us are not able to do so. This is because many of us try to engage in activities where we don't perform well so that we may improve ourselves.

At the same time, we may not engage more and more in the activities where we are naturally gifted. The champions know the best they have and they bring it out whereas many others may not realize the best they have. Hence they may keep trying many other things and in some cases, they may try to succeed in the spheres where they may be the worst.

Hence stop doing things that you are not comfortable with and start doing things that you are most comfortable with; and you may start seeing amazing results. Whether it is physical exercise, profession, relationships or anything else; there are always choices available. Being successful in any one of them is almost equally good in most cases. Success is not about what you do; it is about how you do it.

Hence find the activities that you are most comfortable with and engage in them more and more by increasing the level of resistance. By doing so, you may start seeing amazing results as well as wonderful levels of physical fitness. Learn to be a champion, identify your strengths and start using them to your advantage.

Vices

More and more people have become addicted to various types of vices after 1990. One reason for this increase is that after this time, more and more such products have appeared, which have the potential to cause physical as well as mental damage.

Be it smoking, alcohol, various types of natural and synthetic drugs, excessive physical indulgence in women, especially in the company of paid sex workers; and all other such practices, they all cause damage to the body as well as mind. As the body and mind start losing their potential, the chances of achieving and/or maintaining good things decrease.

All such pleasures need resources. Accordingly, they reduce the amount of positive energy in your aura, since you spend more and more positive energy to avail such resources. Hence you start losing positive energy from your aura. It means you start having less chances of achieving success, unless you keep adding more and more positive energy to your aura by indulging in more and more good karmas and you are able to maintain the balance of positive energy in your aura.

It may seem interesting that many rich people use these things and they're still successful. The primary reasons is that they had big amounts of positive energies in their auras at the beginning of their lives. It means they gathered such energy during their past lives. Looking at the secondary reason; many of them keep collecting fresh positive energy by engaging in a number of good karmas as well as practices. This way, they may be spending less than they may be earning.

Let's try to understand this concept with the help of an example. Suppose there are three individuals and each one of them spends USD 5,000 per month, towards various expenses. Suppose the first person earns USD 8,000 per month, the second one earns USD 5,000 per month and the third one earns USD 3,000 per month. After expenses, the first one will save USD 3,000 per month and the second one will save nothing per month, since his income and expenses are the same. The third one will face a deficit of USD 2,000 per month since his expanses are higher than his income.

He may make up for such deficit as long as he can, through savings, loans and other such media. However, if he keeps doing so, a time may come that it may become difficult to manage such state of affairs and he may face problems. If he has saved money or wealth which he may have got from his parents, he may last longer. However, he may eventually collapse as such savings may be exhausted one day.

It means the first person can still save money after spending so much; the second one may be able to manage and the third one may land into problems if he keeps spending the same amount of money.

It is the same in case of positive energy in the aura. Accordingly, people who have large amounts of positive energy from previous lives may afford to spend more. Some of these people may earn more or much more positive energy in their present lives; than they spend. Hence they may still witness increase in positive energy, despite spending so much of it. However, such increase may be much bigger if they don't spend so much of their energy.

A healthy person can eat lots of sugars but a person with high blood sugar should keep his sugar consumption in check. Here again, the situation is different in case of these two individuals. Hence don't copy others and find out what is suitable according to your situation. If you have vices and they're hindering your growth significantly; it is the time to act.

For some addictions, you may need to go through courses of de-addiction. If such is the case, then get it done. For all other things which you can control on your own, though with difficulty; there are some tips which may help.

For example, if you want to quit smoking, it may not be a good idea to quit it all at once, as the level of resistance may be much more than your conscious ability. Your subconscious has a strong script of 'I want to smoke'. As a result, it may put strong resistance if you try to quit all at once. Hence you should start by reducing the number of cigarettes per day. Suppose you consume 20 cigarettes a day. Trying going for 18 in the beginning.

Once you're comfortable with this level, you may go for 15, 12, 10, 8, 6, 4, 2 and 0 per day. Here again, don't bite more than you can chew since you may end up aggravating your problem. Go slow and have patience. With time and efforts, your subconscious may replace the old script of 'I want to smoke' with 'I don't want to smoke'. With subconscious mind; time and repeated conscious efforts are the most important factors.

In case you consume alcohol in heavy quantities on daily basis; you should try a different approach. You should not try to reduce the amount of alcohol you consume every day. This is because drugs and alcohol weaken your conscious mind as long as they are effective. After a certain quantity of alcohol goes into your body, your conscious mind may not be able to resist. Since there is a strong script of 'I love alcohol' on your subconscious, you may often end up drinking a lot; after you consume a specific quantity of alcohol.

This is why people may speak truth after drinking a lot. The subconscious never lies and it is the conscious which puts filters on what wants to get out. Since the conscious may go very weak after drinking a lot; whatever the subconscious has to offer may get out without any filters. It means the conscious mind may not be able to manipulate and raw truth may get out. For this reason, people may be more trustworthy when they have drunk a lot.

Hence it may not be a good idea to reduce the quantity of alcohol. Instead, you should start by reducing the number of days per week, you consume alcohol. If you consume alcohol every day, reduce one day and stick to 6 days per week for some time. Once you're comfortable with this level, reduce one more day. This way, you may get out of it slowly and surely. Faster you quit; faster you may relapse. Longer you take to quit, less are the chances that you may relapse. With subconscious; speed is almost always your enemy whereas patience and perseverance are you best friends.

Looking at another tip which may help during the initial levels, plan something you love at the same time when you consume alcohol, on your day off. If you don't engage in anything, your subconscious may keep reminding you that this is the time to consume alcohol. As a result, you may find it difficult to stay away from alcohol. Hence use a trick. Engage in something you love to do.

When you do that, your subconscious gets stuck between two things you love. Hence it may get confused and it may not be able to put much resistance. This is because it has to promote what you are doing, due to strong script of liking for such thing written on it. Hence the resistance may decrease and you may cross this level with less difficulty. You can spend your time watching your favourite movie, going out with your girlfriend, spending time on internet, reading a book of your liking or indulging in any other activity that you like a lot.

Once you're comfortable with 6 days a week, you may drop one more day. When you get comfortable with this level also, you're ready to reduce one more day. By this time, your subconscious may have started replacing the old script of 'I love alcohol'. Hence you may not need to engage in special activities when you reach third or fourth level. It means you may follow your regular routines and stay away from alcohol at the same time. From there, you only need more time and effort in order to get out of this problem. Go slow and move to the next level, only when you're duly comfortable with an existing level.

It should be noted that in case of alcohol, you need to control it only if you are using it in heavy quantities, many times a week. However, if you don't drink a lot and you know when to stop, you don't need to bother about getting rid of this habit.

Once again, it varies from individual to individual. Hence you have to find out first, whether the consumption of alcohol is affecting your performance or not. If the answer is yes, start working on it.

Negative Attitude

The Glass is always half Empty

Negative attitude is one of the biggest hurdles on your path to success. Hence you need to act with utmost urgency if you know or find out that you have a negative mindset or negative way of looking at things.

Negative attitude may keep making the conscious and the subconscious mind more and more negative. Accordingly, it can make everything and everyone go away from you as no good things and people can stay with a person who has a highly negative attitude.

Some people having negative attitude may themselves not know that they suffer from this problem. They may think that they are relatively reserved or choosy but not negative in attitude. Let's look at some symptoms which may help in identifying this problem.

The most prominent feature of people with negative attitude is that when they look at people or things, they look for their flaws first. Hence their first opinion about most people or things is negative. Almost all people as well as things have good as well as bad characteristics though some of them may have more good ones and some others may have more bad ones.

A person with positive attitude will almost always look for the positive qualities first whereas a person with negative attitude will almost always spot the negative characteristics first. Some of these people may be so good at being negative that they may be able to spot a negative trait of a person or thing at first look, even if it is the only negative trait that such person or thing may have. You always find what you truly look for. Such people look for negative traits in people and things, with all their hearts, conscious and subconscious minds. Accordingly, they may find negative things only.

In day to day life, you may hear people with negative attitudes saying things like, "look that woman is wearing an out of fashion dress", though the woman may look beautiful in that dress; or "that guy standing in that corner has bad taste in shoes", though the guy may look handsome. Likewise, "look, this new car has some dirt on its bumper", though the car may be otherwise clean.

Similarly, "that girl is not wearing matching pair of shoes", "that guy doesn't know how to shave properly", "this park is so noisy", though it may be a beautiful park; "these kids should not play in front of our house", though it's a common place and all kids play there; "that woman is too short", "that guy is too tall", "your grandma speaks too much", "your grandpa speaks too little", "your brother smiles too much", "your sister smiles too little", "the food is less salty", "the water is too cold" and millions of other such things.

The essence of all these examples is that such people will always look for negative traits in people, things and places, instead of looking for the positive ones. They are good at spotting negative traits and they don't bother much about finding positive traits in people, things or places. This is because through conscious engagement in finding faults, they have written scripts on their subconscious minds to the effect that they only want to look for negative things.

Accordingly, their subconscious minds help them when they try to spot drawbacks or weaknesses. Since they have the supports of their subconscious minds, they may be exceptionally good at finding negative traits. All they really want to see are negative traits and accordingly they see negative traits only.

At times, the negative traits that they may see in people, things or places may not actually be there and they may only perceive that they are there. For this reason, such people may be able to build mountains of negativity out of nothing. Hence if you ask one such person to find 5 bad things about a person, he may do so with ease. However, if you ask him to find 5 good things about a person, you may notice that he's struggling. He may even not be able to succeed despite best conscious effort. If that happens; it means that such person's mindset is highly negative.

Another worth mentioning feature of such people is that many times they speak with negative clauses in their sentences when they may do so with simple positive sentences. For example, if one such person is asked for a choice between tea and coffee, he may say, "I will have coffee as I don't like tea" or "I don't like tea". A person with positive attitude may simply say, "I will have coffee". It means he may not feel the need to mention the fact that he doesn't like tea.

Likewise, one such person can often be found using other negative phrases like, "Out of these two cars, I like the red one as I don't like green colour" instead of simply saying "I like the red one". Looking at another sentence, "I will watch a movie as I don't like watching football" instead of simply saying "I will watch a movie". Similarly, they may use negative clauses in many of their sentences; when simple positive sentences may do the jobs.

Due to negative mindsets, they need to add something negative to each and everything, even if it is a sentence. Hence even if they like something, they may feel the subconscious need to mention something they don't like. They've written strong scripts of finding flaws and criticism on their subconscious minds. Such scripts execute each time they try to do or even say something.

Such is the power of negative mindset. This is why negative attitude is one of the biggest problems that one may face while moving forward with his life. Such people may especially do poorly or very poorly in the sphere of relationships, as they may keep finding faults with the ones who are in relationships with them. As a result, other people may start avoiding them sooner or later.

There are various branches of negative attitude. Some of them are; not trusting other people and even the near ones, doubting most people and even doubting yourself, criticizing other people a lot, finding ways to complain in various spheres of life on account of one reason or another; and other such negative traits which are all rooted in this bigger problem of negative attitude. Hence in order to treat any one of these negative traits, you need to treat the root of these habits which is negative attitude.

As these people have serious lack of trust, it may be difficult for them to trust most people who come in touch with them. Hence they may be poor at relationships. They may not share most of their feelings with others, they may draw boundaries and they may not let people cross those boundaries. As they keep themselves restricted and they don't trust others, they may push most people away from them.

Such mindset may prove especially difficult for a relationship like love affair or marriage. The partner of one such individual may get tired of his constantly doubting attitude, criticism and lack of trust. Hence such individual may face many failed relationships and he may end up being alone in the long run.

Due to the gravity of this problem, it needs to be fixed as soon as you spot it. The root of this problem lies in fear, distrust and inferiority complex. If you have this problem; you are subconsciously afraid that most people and situations may hurt you, exploit you or they may make you feel small. Hence you stop trusting people and you start doubting them. Since others can make you feel small according to you; you start making them smaller by finding faults with them; in order to feel secure. When most things and people around you are flawed, you may feel better in comparison. Hence you start making them smaller so that you may look bigger.

However, it is all happening in your imagination and not in the real world. You can neither make someone bigger nor smaller, as they are what they are. However in the process of making others smaller, you're distancing yourself from them. Everyone is unique and beautiful in their own ways and you just need to see that beauty; even your own beauty.

The habit of comparison is one of the worst habits as it may give birth to baseless fears and insecurities of various types. The fear of getting hurt or being exploited may stop you from playing and it may make you sit on the sidelines. Life is a game and you have to play it as long as you're in it. You'll get hurt at times and you'll get rewarded at times. Embrace everything and keep playing, as all will be well in the end.

Let's see what techniques can help when it comes to rectify negative attitude. You have a subconscious tendency to look for bad in people, things and places. Hence in order to treat your problem in the most effective way, you need to engage in conscious acts of finding beauty in people, things and places. Doing so will start overwriting the script on your subconscious mind. With time and effort, you may finally develop a subconscious habit of seeing beauty in people, things and places. It means you may develop positive attitude.

To begin with, take a scenario where you are alone and no one is with you. This way, no one will judge you and you can take all the time and effort that you need in order to improve yourself. Start with a small activity like opening your social media account 5 to 10 times every day. Look for friends who have updated their status with pictures, thoughts or other types of posts. Start observing them and try to find something good about each one of them or about most of them.

Let's say you start with finding one good thing about some pictures that your friends post and then comment on one such picture with the mention of that good thing. For example, if someone is wearing a good looking shirt, notice it and point it out in your comment which may be something like, "this shade of red suits you a lot" or "you look really good in this shade of blue". Likewise, if a friend is wearing a very good pair of ear rings, notice it and point it out in your comment like, "beautiful picture and especially your ear rings which add to your beauty".

It should be noted that the whole point of doing this activity is to make conscious efforts of finding good things about people, things and places. Hence you should never try this activity with universally proven formal comments like, 'nice pic, beautiful pic, you look nice; or nice'. This is because if you choose to type such comments, you won't engage your conscious mind in any activity. Hence you may not see any results.

However, when you try to find one or two good things in a picture, you will engage your conscious mind in this practice and that is what you need. Though it may seem like an easy job but it is not; as your habit of negative attitude can make it very difficult for you to find good, particularly in the beginning.

For example, when you start with the first picture that someone in your friend list has posted, the first things that you notice may be flaws or negative points in that picture. Don't worry as this is the natural you with the habit of negative attitude. Hence try again and find one good thing or point about that picture and then mention that point in your comment. Though it may take you long to do so with your first few pictures, you have the luxury of all the time you need. In addition to that, no one is there to judge you.

It should be noted that your overall comment should be positive and it should not be a negative one with a positive part like, "oh I love your ear rings though your dress should have been a bit brighter". Similarly, "this red one really suits you a lot though my favourite is green" and other comments like them; where despite the positive thing you noticed and put in, the overall comment is negative.

As you start posting more and more such comments, with each one of these positive comments written after conscious effort of finding beauty in people, places and things; your conscious mind will start sending messages to your subconscious mind that you want to see beauty. Hence slowly but surely, your subconscious mind will start replacing the old script of finding problems in people, which means negative attitude; with the new script of finding beauty in people, which means positive attitude.

As this script gets stronger with your continuous conscious efforts, your subconscious mind may start encouraging as well as helping you. At this point, you may observe that it has become easier for you to notice beauty in people, things and places; and now you need less effort.

Another good thing is that when you start posting beautiful and unique comments about your friends; they may start recognizing that your comments are quite different from usual comments. They'll know that you have taken time to find beautiful things about them and then write them. When that happens, you may start receiving positive vibes of thankfulness from these friends. Such vibes may give big boost to your confidence as you witness that your efforts are being recognized. All you have to do from here is to gain more and more positivity.

An interesting fact about energy is that if you send positive energy to people, you may get positive energy in return whereas if you send negative energy, you may get negative energy in return. It means as you start sending positive energy to your friends, they may send back more and more positive energy which may improve your net energy equation. Hence you may start having better and better energy equation or improved aura with the passage of time.

After some time, you may feel that you have mastered this level. At this point, you may notice that in order to put a beautiful comment on a picture, you don't have to work hard and you don't need much time, since it has started coming easily to you. This is the time when you are ready for the next level. Though the next level may be more challenging, you are likely to be prepared for the increased resistance.

In the next level, start dealing with real life situations and try to find beauty in people, things and places. Since you have already developed a habit of giving complements and finding good in people, places and things, it should not be difficult for you to do so. Start with simple but true complements that appreciate the people you meet.

For example, you can say, "Oh Anna, this red dress looks really good on you and by the way, red is my favourite colour too" or "Mr. Smith, this new hair style gives you quite a different look, in a good way". Likewise, "Your apartment is really impressive and I especially like your living room" or "Oh, you're going on a vacation to Europe; It's beautiful and you'll surely love it" and other such complements which are honest and positive.

One thing that you have to keep in mind while engaging in these activities is that your complements should involve conscious effort and they must be honest. For example, if you don't like red, don't say that red is your favourite colour, merely in order to make the complement better. In this case, simply say, "Red looks really good on you".

Always remember that sooner or later, people will get to know whether your efforts are real or fake. Hence always make real and honest efforts. As you keep telling good things to other people, most people you complement may start being friendlier with you. Some of them may also start doing small favours for you, which may increase your faith in them. Hence you may start trusting people more and more, as you find out that there are many good qualities in them and they wish well for you.

While you are consciously working to get rid of negative attitude, you should absolutely stay away from such people around you who may have the same habit. This is a must follow rule and it is so important that even if your own mother, father, brother, sister, best friend or your spouse is seriously affected by this habit, you should avoid their company until you've gained a fair amount of positive energy through various practices.

People with negative attitudes are highly likely to have negative auras. Hence they may transfer negative energy to your aura through their company as well as interactions. At early stages, negative energy coming to you is the last thing you want if you wish to get rid of this habit. It is like you don't sit with your friends while they're consuming alcohol, if you're trying to quit drinking.

Once you have achieved a good level of positive attitude, you can choose to be with selective people with negative attitude like your close relatives or friends. Even at this stage, you should avoid people with negative attitude who you can afford to avoid. The kind of company you keep on regular basis and the kind of people you deal with on regular basis is an important factor in making you a positive or a negative person. Accordingly, you should choose wisely who you spend your time with, as it is an important factor in giving you more good habits or more bad habits.

While going through this practice, as much as you may benefit by staying away from negative people, you may benefit the same or more by keeping company with more and more people with positive attitudes. More time you spend in the company of such people, more positive energy may come to you. Accordingly; you may find it easier to get rid of your habit of negative attitude.

The company of people with strong positive mindsets is really very helpful in such cases as such people may provide you with lots of positive energy and motivation. At the same time, you may get to engage in more and more positive activities in their company. This is because engaging in more and more positive activities is what people with strong positive mindsets do, most of the time.

As the practice of finding beauty in people continues and as you start doing it more often, you may find out that a stage has reached where you don't have to do much conscious effort to spot beauty or good in people and then complement them. At this stage, the first thing that may come to your mind when you see a person, thing or place is a beautiful or good thing about them. This is exactly the opposite of what it was before; which was negative things coming to your mind whenever you saw people, things or places. It means your negative attitude has gone and you can build up from here, more and more.

Remember that most people, things and places have good as well as bad traits in them as no one and nothing is perfect. However, whether you see beauty or ugliness in them, doesn't define them and it defines you. If you see beauty in them, you're beautiful inside. If you see ugliness in them; ugliness is what lies within you. It is like whatever is the colour of the goggles you wear; the same may be projected on everything you see.

It means everything may appear greenish to you if you wear dark green goggles. Likewise, everything may look blackish to you, if you're wearing black goggles. Beauty and ugliness are relative and they lie in the eye of the beholder. Hence you'll always see beauty if you're beautiful inside. If you're not able to see beauty; try not to fix the objects in your vision; and try to fix your vision. Heaven or hell is all about your point of view or mindset and nothing else.

Isn't it a small but surprising example of the mindset of different people that if you keep a glass half filled with water and then ask different people what does the glass look like, you may get different answers. Some may say that the glass is half filled whereas some others may say that the glass is half empty.

In reality, the glass is half filled as well has half empty. The ones who see the glass as half filled have positive mindsets. Hence they notice that the glass is half filled. The ones who see the glass as half empty have negative mindsets. Hence they spot emptiness first. Whatever their answers may be; such answers don't tell much about the glass and they tell about them. An empty person may see the empty part whereas a filled person may see the filled part. Hence it's not about how the glass is or should be and it is about how you are or should be.

It means people, places and things won't change in most cases. It is you who has to change and this change means the change in your attitude or mindset. Yes, there will always be some people or things which won't work well for you or which won't suit you even if you have strong positive attitude. However, such people or things are not many in numbers. You may discover that as your mindset gets more and more positive, the number of hurtful people may decrease in the same proportion.

This is because good and bad are relative. When you really want to see ugliness in people, you'll bring out their ugly parts. On the other hand, you'll bring out their beautiful parts if all you want to see is the beauty in them. For this reason, the same person may be good for someone whereas he may be bad for someone else.

Though the person in question remains the same; the other one has changed. It means if he's bad for someone, that someone may also do things to bring evil out of this person. It means that the other person himself may not be very good or good. Likewise, if the person in question is good for someone else; that someone may also do things to bring the best out of this person. It means that the other person in this case may himself be good or very good.

All heavenly pleasures come from within your mind, they encourage you to do good things, you do so and you benefit. Likewise, all evil also rises from within you, it encourages you to do bad things, you do so and you suffer. Though you may engage in good things in the first case and in bad things in the second case; one thing is common in both these situations. You have only achieved what you really wanted to achieve. The world around you changes as you change because everything is relative.

When a drop of water falls into mud, it becomes mud. If the same drop of water falls on a lotus, it shines like a pearl. If the same drop of water falls into the mouth of an oyster, it may actually become a pearl. Though the drop of water is the same in all cases, the result is different in each case, depending on who receives this drop of water.

People are like this drop of water and in most cases, it all depends on what you want to get out of them. If you choose to be mud, you may get mud in return. If you choose to be lotus, you may get bright shining results from people. If you choose to be an oyster, you may get beautiful results like pearls from the same people.

Though such stage is difficult to reach and it may take you long to reach this stage, it can finally be reached. Hence you should start walking towards this goal of having a highly positive aura or a highly positive attitude. As you cover more and more distance on the path of positivity, more and more beautiful and amazing rewards may be delivered to you. Accordingly, you may be in a better position to enjoy life to the fullest, by spreading good things and getting good things in return.

Most people are mixtures of good as well as evil and they may serve as a mirror to you. Hence if you are beautiful yourself, you may see a beautiful picture of yourself in them whereas if you are ugly, you may see an ugly picture of yourself in them. In simple words, if you choose to do beautiful things to people, they may return them with beautiful things and hence the picture looks beautiful.

Though you may think that this beautiful picture is theirs but in reality, this picture is yours because people are only reflecting the same beauty that originated from within you. Hence this is your own beautiful picture. On the other hand, if you choose to do ugly things to people, they may also return them with ugly things. In this case, your picture looks ugly when seen in the mirror of people. Here again, the mirror is not to blame and you are.

Therefore, stop blaming or cleaning the mirror if you are not able to see a beautiful picture of yourself in it. Recognize the fact that in order to look beautiful in the mirror, you will actually need to be beautiful. Hence start doing it at the earliest.

Too Many Fears, Lack of Confidence

Though lack of confidence is not as bad as negative attitude, it is still capable of taking so much away from you; especially the big things. This is because all big things almost always need great amount of confidence as well as an undivided faith that you can achieve them, which is not there if you lack confidence.

Lack of confidence is a problem of the subconscious, which says you are not fit to accomplish big tasks. As the intensity of this problem increases; even small goals may become difficult to achieve as you may have very low confidence. Let's look into the root cause of this problem as the best solution always comes from the root. This is because once we know where the root of a problem lies, it is easier to treat it and remove it.

First of all, let's see what confidence is. It is a feeling that you have what it takes to accomplish a particular objective. Confidence is a collective result of a number of qualities you may possess. Taking an example, suppose you're to deliver speech in English which is not your mother language. This piece of speech is related to a topic of science and the size of the audience is about 500 people.

In order to be confident that you'll get through, you need three major variables working in your favour. First of all, you must be good at the topic you're going to speak about. Secondly, you should be good in English as otherwise, you may not speak fluently. Thirdly, you must be comfortable speaking before an audience of 500 people. If you have all these things under your belt; you may feel confident about your performance. If one or more than one of them is missing, you may not feel confident.

This is how it works in general where confidence is dependent on a number of variables involved in a particular equation. Some of these variables may be real whereas some may be projected by your fears. In the recent example; being good at the topic you're going to speak about is the most essential variable and you can't afford to miss it. Hence if you don't know much about the topic, you may lack confidence and this feeling is real.

The second and relatively less essential variable is your command over English. Even if you are not very good at English, you can still convey your message; provided you know a lot about the topic you're going to speak about. Hence this variable is partly essential and partly made up by your mind.

Looking at the third variable which is the comfort to speak before an audience, this is completely made up and no part of it is real. This is because an audience in reality has nothing to do with whether or not you know the topic and/or English. The fear of audience is all made up by your mind. It means you can deliver a wonderful speech even if it is your first time before an audience. Likewise, you may fail to deliver if you fear audience; even if you've done it dozens of times.

Hence lack of confidence may have a number of contributing factors; some of which may be real and some may be made up. As far as the real ones are concerned, the best way to fix them is by having them. It means you must learn the topic you're going to speak about; and there may be no way around it. However in many cases, the imaginary and not the real factors cause the problems. For instance, most people won't consider delivering speech on subjects they know nothing about. It means they may consider such topics only if they are good at them. Hence the decision of whether or not they are good at one such topic is not difficult to make and it is made on merit.

When it comes to the imaginary part; most people suffering from lack of confidence fail there. The fear of performance is not real and it is imaginary. For instance, you may deliver your first speech before an audience and you may perform wonderfully. It means if you fear that you may not be able to perform before an audience, such fear is not based on real facts and it is imaginary. Hence this part of the problem needs maximum attention.

This is because you'll perform one thing or another for the first time, throughout your life, as there's always a first time for everything. If you're afraid of doing it, you may not engage in it and it may always remain the thing you've not tried. Let's see how this attitude may build the problem of lack of confidence.

Suppose an individual tries something for the first time and he fails. Based on his mindset, he may broadly take two paths. Looking at the first path, he may not bother much about it and he may keep trying until he succeeds. It means he has positive mindset and he understands that failures are a part of the learning curve. Hence he's not bothered by failures and he keeps doing what he wants; even if he fails.

Though this individual may not perform this task well for a number of times, he's confident that he will, in the end. If you're this person, lack of confidence is not your problem.

Looking at the second path, he may get afraid that he won't be able to perform this task well. Hence he may get afraid of attempting it again. It means he has a weak positive aura or a negative aura. Hence he may choose not to try such task again; unless it is something he can't avoid. He tries a number of other tasks as we all do; and he fails at some of them. This gives rise to another type of fear. The first one is that he may not perform well at a particular task and the second one is that he may not perform well at things he's doing for the first time.

As that happens, he may try to avoid doing things for the first time as he's afraid that he may fail. Through all such conscious acts, he may write script on the subconscious that he's afraid of trying new things and he's not comfortable with tasks which he's not skilled at. This gives rise to a big problem since the only way to be good at doing something is through practice. Unless you've done something repeatedly, you may not be good or very good at it. Though some people may need less practice and some may need more; everyone needs practice.

Once you've reached this stage, your problem may become serious. This is because you don't want to attempt things that you're not comfortable with and the only way to get comfortable with them is by doing them over and over again. It means you're stuck. Your subconscious warns you not to try new things due to fear of failure and you can't succeed until you try again and again.

Such fear of failure is the root cause of lack of confidence. It may not let you try new things and you may end up lacking confidence more and more. This is because more you feed this feeling of 'I can't do it', stronger it gets. Stronger it gets, more you may feel that you can't do it. It means the cause starts feeding the effect and the effect starts feeding the cause. Hence you're stuck in a vicious cycle where fear of failure aggravates lack of confidence and lack of confidence aggravates fear of failure.

In its deepest sense, confidence is not knowing that you'll succeed if you keep trying. It is a feeling that all you need to do is try and give your best. Whatever the results may be, you're not bothered. Hence a truly confident person may play football for fun, he may not play well even after years and he may still enjoy it. Even after years of being a bad player or not so good player, you ask him to play football and he's in before you know.

It means though he may not perform well, he's confident about playing. Hence in the deepest sense, he knows that his job is to try and not to succeed or fail. With this approach, nothing can take away your confidence because you're focused on the act and not on the results. When the worst results can't shake you, what else can? The beauty of such attitude is that in most cases, you'll succeed. This is because it is fear of failure that puts a lot of pressure on you and affects your performance. If you're not afraid of failure, the pressure is lifted and you may perform a lot better, succeeding in most cases.

Hence in order to completely fix the problem of lack of confidence, you don't need to make sure that you'll win if you keep trying. If you think about victory, you're still focused on results, which means the pressure of performance is still there. Hence if you don't succeed at a task even after doing it dozens of times; you may start fearing that you may not succeed at it all, no matter how hard you may try.

It means this is not the best approach though it may be the second best. There are three options here. The first one is that you don't try because of fear of failure; and it is the worst option. The second one is that you convince yourself that you'll succeed if you keep trying despite failures. It is a much better approach but it is not the best approach. This is because you're still fixed on the results of your karmas, which takes the focus away from the karmas. It means you're focused on the destination and you're not able to focus on the path. Since the path alone may take you to destination, such distraction may prove costly.

Therefore with this approach, you may try again if you fail. However, if you fail repeatedly at a task, you may quit it, since you don't want to fail in the end. This approach is certainly much better than the first one where you choose not to try at all. However with this approach, you may not achieve the best possible results since you may still not address the root cause of your problem which is fear of failure.

In the deepest sense, fear of failure can't be fixed by winning again and again; though it can be treated and kept under control through this practice. This is because you have to lose every now and then, since no one can win at everything. As and when you fail, the fear may come back and you may have to suppress it by winning again, in some other field. Hence the second option may keep it under control but it may not fix the problem.

The third option is the best fix for fear of failure. The moment you learn to welcome failure as well as you welcome success; your problem is fixed. At this stage, you may perform poorly at something but you may still be confident when you attempt it. Hence you may be confident despite failures. It means your confidence is not dependent on success and failure any longer. You've learnt this valuable lesson that all you need to do is try and give your best. Whatever the outcomes may be, let them be.

Once you reach this stage, nothing can shake you or your confidence. The beauty of this stage is that you may succeed at most things you attempt since you're focused on the acts and not on the results. Such focus improves your efforts, since you're not distracted or divided. As a result, you perform better; and better performance means better chances of success. It means that in the deepest sense, the one who doesn't bother whether he wins or loses and he only believes in playing; wins the most.

Let's see how the problem of lack of confidence may be fixed. Since the subconscious has registered a script of running away from difficult situations, it may discourage you when you try to engage in such situations. The visible effect of such discouragement is lack of confidence. Hence you need to replace this script with 'I can do it' or 'I don't care if I fail'. If you choose 'I can do it', you're going for the second option. If you choose, 'I don't care if I fail', you're going for the third and the best option.

Though everyone may wish to take the best option, it may not prove good for most people who are currently going with the first option; that of 'I can't do it'. This is because switching from the first to the third option directly may prove very difficult for most people. Hence it is better to upgrade yourself to 'I can win' first and then upgrade to 'I don't care if I fail'. This is because you're fed up of failures and you may want some wins to gain momentum. Hence going for the second option may prove better.

Let's look at some activities which can help you in treating this problem. Start with small tasks which are not difficult and at the same time, they are the ones that you have not tried at all. For example, choose an easy-to-play game on a computer or a video game and start playing it. It should be noted that in order to make the most of this activity, you should start engaging in such acts on your own in the first step. Avoid involvement of other people. When you play against a person, your fear of losing and feeling embarrassed may be much stronger compared to when you're playing against computer, since no one is there to judge you.

You should start with the game that you find the easiest; even if have to play a number of games in order to find out which one is the easiest one for you. Various people are comfortable with different types of activities. Accordingly, they have better chances of performing at their best in different activities. Hence you should choose a game that you really like and find easy.

As you start completing more and more levels of such game with conscious efforts, your conscious mind starts sending more and more messages to your subconscious mind. As your subconscious mind receives more and more messages of success, it may send fewer fears. Hence you may gain some confidence. With time and efforts, you may feel comfortable with this level and the feeling of 'I can do it' may be there whenever you try to play. It means you're ready for the next level.

If you don't like playing video games or computer games, you can choose other activities like walking, jogging, running, swimming, going to gym, cycling, rope skipping, aerobics, yoga or any other such activities. Here again, choose the one that you feel the most comfortable with and then start doing it with increased levels of resistance, introduced after regular intervals of time. For example, if you find that you are the most comfortable with running, start with one mile or less without stopping. Then move up from there on regular basis like adding half a mile or so, every week or every couple of weeks.

Apart from physical activities, some other types of activities can also help you achieve the same goal. For example, you may learn a new language, learn and remember complete lyrics of more and more songs, learn and remember poems, learn and practice cooking dishes, learn and remember more and more about places of significance, learn and remember about great people in history of mankind, learn and remember valuable quotes and sayings as well as their meanings, learn and practice new skills like sewing, painting, writing, singing, playing guitar, playing piano and a wide variety of other such activities.

If you choose to learn something that needs to be remembered or practiced like lyrics of songs and cooking new dishes, you should not simply learn and disengage as that won't complete the task. Hence you should repeat such practices so that you are consciously doing them again and again. Through such repeated conscious efforts, you will send more and more signals to your subconscious mind where these signals may say, "I can do it and I can do it again and again".

The reason that video games or computer games are better is that they require maximum conscious effort from your mind. Since this problem is of the mind, engaging in practices which require more effort from your mind than your body may do this job in far less time. In addition to that, games come with a number of benefits. Playing games requires conscious mental effort and they may increase your concentration, as concentration is the first thing you need to play most games. Next advantage is that games are relatively easy though effective, when compared to physical activities like running or cycling which require a lot of physical activity. Accordingly, you may not like them much; especially in the beginning.

Apart from that, playing games is one activity that you can do for hours and hours whereas you can engage in many other activities like running or cycling, or learning to cook new dishes, only for relatively short periods of time every day. Above all these things, playing such games may sharpen your mental abilities day by day as such games require most of the effort from your end, in form of mental effort. As a basic rule, more you practice with any part of your body or mind, stronger it gets.

Have you wondered why young or very young kids of new generations are much better than we were at their ages when it comes to mental abilities? The reason is that through the introduction of various gadgets and through the revolution of the internet, the kids of new generations are getting smarter and smarter in terms of mental abilities. This is because they are practicing and exercising their mental abilities far more than we did at their ages. As they use their mental abilities more and more, they are smarter.

Another trick that can increase the pace of your recovery is to play games that feature small rounds compared to the games which are long and continuous. The primary objective of playing these games is to send more and more messages of, "I can do it", to your subconscious mind. That will happen only once you complete a round or mission. When you play games that feature small rounds or levels, you may be able to send more signals to your subconscious mind. You may complete a round every 2 to 5 minutes. This message of completion is what will do the trick, when it is forwarded to your subconscious mind.

Hence avoid playing such games in the beginning, where it may take you 20 or 30 minutes to complete a round. Memorize this fact that each time you want to change the script written on your subconscious mind, you need more and more messages. Accordingly, you should target activities which keep giving you messages of success every now and then. This way, you may be able to send a bigger number of messages in relatively less amount of time. Subconscious is a creature of habit and it loves nothing more than repetition. Hence the quantum of each individual success may not matter as much to your subconscious as the number of such occurrences may.

Apart from that, each time you win in any sphere of life, regardless of whether such win is big or small, you gain more confidence and strength to win the next time. For this reason also, you should increase the number of messages which say 'mission accomplished'.

To speed up the process, engage in more than one such activity every day. This may ensure that you are not addicted to only one type of activity. Engaging in more and more activities means having more wins. Doing so may give your confidence a greater boost and you may become better at many things. As more and more messages are sent to your subconscious, it may pose less resistance and you may feel comfortable with the first level. Once that happens, you should move to the second level.

In the next level, start doing the opposite of the first level where you chose activities which were new for you. Instead, choose activities from various spheres of life, where you have comfort and start engaging in such activities more and more. Since you have achieved a reasonable level of confidence, you are ready to deal with real things: things that can bring you success and appreciation.

When you start engaging in one such activity, choose the one that you find yourself most comfortable with. This way, you may achieve more in relatively short period of time as well as with relatively less effort.

You may choose to improve your professional skills at this level. Try those spheres where you feel the maximum comfort so that you may gain more and more confidence through repeated occurrences of success. Keep in mind that you should not engage in such spheres at this stage, where you don't feel comfortable. For example, it may be a bad idea to open a food joint if you don't know much about cooking and/or managing. Your confidence is building at this stage and you don't want to push it back by facing failures.

If you have the luxury to change your field of profession, change it if you don't have much comfort in your existing profession. Even if you earn somewhat less in the new field, it's worth taking the chance if you have very good comfort level in such field. Since you like your new job, you may feel comfortable and comfort means more success. More success means more appreciation. Hence you may gain more confidence through more success and appreciation. Remember, it doesn't matter what you do and how you do it is what matters.

During the first and second level, you should stay away from people with lack of confidence and those with negative attitudes. The energy transferred by these people can make it difficult for you to get rid of your problem of low confidence. Taking an example, one such person may bring your confidence down by saying, "I once tried a couple of courses of personality development to gain confidence but despite months of hard work, none of them worked". Imagine how much damage such a line can do to your confidence at this stage.

Hence avoid the company of such people and instead, keep company with people who are confident and who have positive mindsets. They may transfer a lot of positive energy to you and they may also encourage you to achieve more through your efforts. Some of them may even quote some incidences which may help you a lot in moving forward. For instance, one such person may say, "I also went low on confidence at one point in life. However, I fought back and got everything in order'. Imagine how much motivation such incident may provide. Hence keep company with positive and confident people. You may see them achieve new heights every day; and that may motivate you to do the same. Such people are living examples of 'I can do it'.

Apart from that, reading or watching life stories of people who achieved great things by virtue of sheer courage and confidence may also help you gain more confidence. You may find that many of these people suffered from failures and setbacks again and again. However, they kept moving and they reached. This may motivate you to keep moving ahead, despite failures and setbacks.

It should be noted that such stories may be used to provide extra boost and you can't improve merely by reading or watching them and not engaging in any efforts. Memorize this fact that your subconscious is smart enough to differentiate between thoughts generated as results of actions and plain thoughts. Hence it may pay due attention to a thought or feeling which is generated after accomplishing a task. However, it may ignore a feeling or thought if it is generated without action or if it is not followed by action; and you're trying to fool yourself with words alone. Hence engaging in conscious acts is the most important part.

Another point to keep in mind is that you should move slowly. Remember, speed is your enemy whereas patience and perseverance are your best friends on this journey. Hence don't get carried away by motivational speeches or biographies and try to attempt a task which may be much bigger than your potential at a point in time. If you do so, you may fail miserably. Such failure may not only shake your confidence, it may also make you lose faith in motivational speeches and biographies. Therefore, move step by step.

Personality development is like raising a building. Consolidate your foundations first, through specifically targeted activities. Keep doing them over and over again until you have made your foundations strong enough to hold the building. Then start building the structure, all the way from bottom to top, slowly and steadily. This is the best mantra for success and you should stick to it if you wish to raise a flag of excellence on top of a building of success, the building of your success.

Once you've mastered the second level, you may proceed to the next one. In this level, try attempting tasks which you have not tried, which you don't feel comfortable with and/or which may be new and difficult. Even if you witness initial setbacks, you should be fine since you've achieved a lot by this time. As you succeed in some of them after initial failures; your confidence may gain more strength. This is the time you may realize that despite initial failures, you may succeed if you keep trying. You may build up more and more from here.

Though you can try to achieve the third option of 'I don't care if I fail' once you've perfected the second option of 'I can do it'; it is an advanced option. Hence we'll not discuss details of this option here, since it is more helpful for people who wish to work more for spiritual growth than materialistic growth.

For material growth; second option works best for most people. However, a mixture of second and third option may prove even better. It means you attempt to achieve every goal you fix and if you fail; you accept and move on.

Lack of Discipline

One thing you can't bring back is the time that has passed.

Though the habit of lack of discipline may not be as damaging as habits like negative attitude and lack of confidence, it can still cause problems in various spheres of your life.

You may be able to manage your life with occasional bumps and hurdles, even if you lack discipline, as long as you aspire to achieve objectives up to the middle level. In case you're a loaded with a number of positive qualities, you may even go up to upper middle level.

Hence if all you wish to achieve is a decent job, a decent car, a decent apartment, a good looking life partner and other such things and people which match this level, you may do so without much discipline. However, if you're interested in results falling in upper class or top class; you may not get most of them with lack of discipline. Even if you get some of them despite lacking discipline, such results may not sustain and you may lose them.

Search through the history of mankind and you will find that all great achievers in various spheres of life had great sense of discipline. In every sphere, the competition at the top level is always the toughest. In order to survive such competition and succeed, you can't afford to have many weaknesses. Lack of discipline is one habit which may prove very troublesome, if you're aiming for top results.

Look into the lives of all self-made and successful people. You may find that these people manage their affairs with great discipline. They organize activities like eating, working, meeting others, relaxing and other activities very well, so that they are able to manage their day to day affairs in impressive and timely manners.

Speaking about time, management of time is one of the most favourite things among successful people. Effective time management is one of the best forms of discipline and it is very important if you want to reach the top and stay there. This is because at top levels of competition, time is of great value. If there is one thing that successful people have less than an average man, it is time.

Most of us love those things the most, which we like and which at the same time are available in limited quantities. Have you ever wondered why billions of people wait for a football world cup or cricket world cup event? This is because they love football or cricket very much and such an event comes after four or five years. During such four or five years, the hunger or thirst reaches its peak. Hence they love such events.

If you get to be in the company of Angelina Jolie or Brad Pitt or any one of your favourite stars for a day; you may enjoy it like crazy. However, if Brad and Angelina spend a day together in the same manner like you did with one of them, their levels of joy may not be the same, though they may have a very good day. The reason is that though they may like each other much more than you like anyone of them, they get to meet each other a lot. Accordingly, they may not be as crazy for each other as you may be for one of them, because their desire for each other is taken care of, on regular basis.

Hence the things or people we like the most and at the same time, we are not able to get much of them; are the ones we value the most. Thus the richest and the most successful people value time the most, since they don't have much of it. If you ask a billionaire for help in form of money, he may not be bothered much. However, if you ask him for a week or even a day of his life, you are likely to make him speechless. Likewise, if you ask the Prime Minister or President of your country for a decent job or an election ticket, he may be able to manage it. However, if you ask him to give you a week of his time, you may find him speechless too.

This is because majority of successful people have such abilities and talents that they can achieve much more than they are currently achieving, if they have more time to do many more things. Since they don't have the extra time, they have to make the most of the time they have on their hands. Time is of utmost value if you want to reach at the top and stay there.

Lack of management of time and/or space is lack of discipline. It means if you have this habit, you may manage your time and/or affairs poorly or not properly. Even if you don't manage your affairs properly, you're ultimately losing time. This is because life is limited and you're wasting it; which means you're wasting time. For instance, if it takes you 1 month to accomplish a task with due discipline and 3 months without much discipline, you've wasted 2 months if you chose to do it without discipline. Hence you need to fix this problem at the earliest.

In order to do so, the first thing you need is effective time management. You can begin by making daily schedules for yourself. Taking an example, suppose you are doing a job which allows you only two hours of free time in the evening and Saturday as well as Sunday as free day. Plan your non-official tasks in a way that you may do them effectively in your free time. Hence, instead of avoiding some compulsory shopping on Saturday or Sunday and then taking a leave or half day on the next Tuesday or Wednesday for the same shopping, learn to do such shopping during weekend. Doing so may save you time as well as trouble.

Memorize this fact that if you want to achieve best results in profession, you'll need to put work on high priority. Hence you should not stay away from work due to issues in your personal life, where such issues have been created due to poor management of time. There are times when you need to take time off from work due to important personal reasons. Such breaks are fine, since personal life is equally important. However, don't mess up in your personal life and then try to compensate by taking time from your profession. Manage your personal affairs in a way that they don't have negative impact on your performance at work.

Looking at the broader definition of lack of discipline, you have it if you fail to comply with some rules or codes which may be compulsory in order to manage your day to day affairs in the best possible manner. If you fail to comply with these rules, you lack discipline. Lacking discipline may keep you away from the best results in most spheres of life. Hence you need to fix this habit.

Looking at the root of this problem, you may have consciously avoided certain codes or rules in the beginning.

Such acts sent messages to your subconscious mind that it's fine if you didn't comply with rules. You might not have had big goals to achieve at that time. Hence you might not have suffered much, even if you didn't comply. Hence you might have continued this practice consciously. With time and repetition, you wrote a script of 'I don't care about discipline', on your subconscious mind.

Once such script is formed, the subconscious starts executing it. At this stage, you don't need to consciously avoid necessary rules or codes; you start avoiding them naturally which means subconsciously. It means you've developed a habit of lacking discipline. Hence you may engage in a number of such activities in your day to day life; which may lack discipline.

Taking an example, coming home at night and parking your car on the road outside your house when you have proper parking space in your garage and you don't have plans to go anywhere before the next morning is lack of discipline. Similarly, taking your shirt off and leaving it on sofa instead of putting it at its proper place is lack of discipline. Having your dinner sometimes at 9, sometimes at 10 and sometimes even at 11 in the evening, even when you return home from your office at 8 PM on daily basis is lack of discipline.

Leaving the gas tank of your car empty at night when you could easily get it filled on the way home, knowing that this is the only car you have in case of an emergency, is lack of discipline. Not emptying your garbage bin for days, even if it is full of junk and you only need to walk a few steps to empty it, is lack of discipline. Not polishing your shoes in the evening when you know that you need to leave early in the morning for an important job and you need to wear these shoes, not reaching for most of your appointments on time, not completing your tasks in time, not arriving at your job on time, spending more than your income, not following proper daily routines of eating, bathing, working, relaxing and many other such things constitute the habit of lack of discipline.

It means in the deepest sense, discipline is not a law that someone or some system imposes on you. It is a set of rules or codes which may change with change in situations; and you make and/or obey these rules in order to manage your affairs effectively as well as in timely manner. Hence having discipline is saving time and unnecessary troubles.

In order to treat this problem, start from the bottom and then build up as always. Start putting conscious efforts to make sure that you complete the aforementioned activities and/or other likewise activities in discipline manner. As you do that again and again, your conscious mind may replace the old script of 'I don't care about discipline or rules' to 'I love discipline', written on your subconscious mind. Once that happens, you've got rid of lack of discipline.

Never attempt tasks which are much bigger than your potential at any point in time. Assess your situation and undertake tasks accordingly. For best results, such tasks should offer resistance which should be somewhat more than you can handle but not a lot more than you can handle. Hence you should engage in small activities in the beginning, like the aforementioned ones.

On the other hand, you should avoid big activities like undertaking a big work project and committing to yourself that you'll finish it within time. Though such task may be accomplished with some resistance during the third or fourth level; it may be too much to handle during the first level. Hence choose your tasks wisely.

Bad Company or Little Company

Planets keep company with stars and hence they shine without having any light.

The kind of company you keep has major impact on whatever you achieve or become in life. Though planets don't have light of their own, they shine as they keep company with stars and reflect their light.

Having bad company is one such negative habit which may destroy all your positive habits with time. Lions keep company with lions and not with jackals. People on the path of divinity don't keep company with corrupted people as the latter may corrupt them also. Wise men keep company with the wise and they don't keep company with fools. A wise man may seldom get any wisdom from a fool whereas he may learn useless things which may diminish his wisdom.

Likewise, brave keep company with brave, intelligent keep company with intelligent and a number of other type of people keep company with similar type of people. This is because all such people need specific types of positive energies to maintain and/or increase their specific abilities. The best sources of such specific energies are the people who have similar interests and some of whom may be more advanced in their relative fields. It means a wise man may become wiser if he keeps company with people who are wiser than him or who are wise in general. This way, they may share similar types of energies and each one of them may benefit.

On the other hand, if you keep company with people who have specific types of negative energies which are the opposites of those that you have, you may witness significant reduction in your positive energies. This is because such negative energies may specifically counteract your positive energies. Taking an example, suppose you start spending time in the company of someone who is lazy and selfish whereas you are active and kind.

Laziness lies in opposition to activeness; and selfishness is the opposite of kindness. It means these two specific energies in his aura may try to counteract two specific energies in your aura. The converse is also true. It means his aura may try to make you lazy and selfish whereas your aura may try to make him active and kind. If your aura is much stronger than his, one such person may not be much of an issue.

However, if your aura is not that strong and/or if you keep company with a number of such people; you may start losing your positive energy. Looking at real life incidents, you may wish to engage in activities and such friend may wish to relax. You may wish to engage in acts of kindness whereas he may tell you and show you otherwise. If this continues, it may cause problems for you.

Likewise, for each positive quality of yours, there may be people who have negative qualities lying exactly opposite to such quality. When you keep company with a number of people who have negative auras; they may counteract most of your positive energies. Some of them may lack confidence, some may lack courage, some may be greedy, some may be selfish, some may be lazy, some may lack discipline and some may have negative attitudes. Hence together they may cause serious damage to your aura. Therefore, it is wise to stay away from company of negative people and keep company with positive people.

Positive people may have various types of positives energies which may make them kind, active, disciplined, courageous, wise, intelligent and confident among many other things. Hence you may gain such energies through their auras as well as through activities that you may perform in their company. For example, you may learn to be more disciplined in the company of someone who's duly disciplined. Likewise, you may become more courageous in the company of someone who's courageous. The same holds for most other positive qualities.

Therefore, it is the time to analyze the kind of company you keep. If you find out that negative people in your circle are higher or much higher in number than positive people, it is the time to act. Get rid of as many of them as many you can. At the same time, keep looking for people with positive auras and add such people to your circle. Doing so may significantly improve your chances of being a better person. Remember, a man is recognized by the company he keeps.

There may still be some negative people in your circle who you can't afford to get rid of. Such people may include close relatives or childhood friends who share a lifetime of experiences with you. Hence it may be selfish to break up with them. However, you can make sure that the number of positive people in your circle is much higher than that of negative people. As far as close relatives and friends are concerned, try to help them become positive. This way, they'll improve and as they improve, you also gain since the number of positive people around you increases and that of negative people decreases.

Another habit which may prove troublesome is that of having little company. It means you don't have healthy amount of people in your circle, including your close relatives and friends. If this is your problem, start working on it and make new friends. The world is full of various types of positive people and you can't afford the luxury of missing most of them. As you add more and more positive people to your circle, you may gain more and more positive energy. Since various people may carry different types of positive energies, they may add many types of positive energies to your aura; through their company as well as through activities.

In order to begin this practice, simply start interacting with more and more people. For example, start interacting with your office colleagues, your neighbors, your school or college mates, parents of your son or daughter's friends and many other such people who keep meeting you from time to time but you really don't do much effort to catch up with them. You may think that most of these people are not worthy of being your friends. However, you should give each one of them fair chances so that you may get to know them better.

You may find out that many of these people are good or very good but they were reserved, just like you. Hence you couldn't see their inner sides from distance. However, once you got closer, you witnessed a number of positive shades in their characters. Hence start such interactions by taking a step forward. Many of them may be good but hesitant to make the first move. Interact with them and then decide.

Keep the ones you find worthy and leave the ones who are negative.

This process may be hard and tiring in the beginning but the rewards may be well worth the efforts. Suppose you interact with 10 people and you are able to add only one good person to your circle. If it so happens, even then you're benefitting. You only need to interact with each one of 9 people 2-4 times before you decide to move away on merit. However, the one person that you've gained through the process may stay with you and enrich you for the rest of your life. Hence on this path; failures don't repeat whereas success stories do.

Therefore, if you need 10 good friends, all you need to do is interact with about 100 people; spread over a period of time. With time and effort, you may have more positive people around you and you may all benefit from one another.

Hence start interacting with people and begin this beautiful journey of making more friends. During this journey, take those people with you whom you find good and positive enough to be your friends and leave those people behind who are only likely to pull you back through the negativity they have.

Lack of Courage

Lack of courage means you have specific types of fears which discourage you from engaging in activities which involve elements of risk. Hence you want to play safe.

Since everything involves risk though some activities may involve high risk and some may involve low risk, this habit may prove troublesome. It may prove more troublesome if you wish to achieve big things in life; since most big things involve big risks.

At times, lack of courage may be confused with lack of confidence. They may seem the same but they are different, though similar. Lack of confidence is a feeling of fear that you don't have what it takes to do a job whereas lack of courage is a feeling that you may suffer losses if you fail. Generally, they both come in pair, since one of them aggravates the other. Taking an example, you may be very good and confident as a teacher but you may be afraid of attempting physically risky tasks. Hence you may have confidence in many spheres but you may lack courage.

For instance, you may be confident that you don't want to go for mountain tracking. You may be afraid that you may end up hurting yourself and hence you choose to abstain. You may be confident in your decision but you may lack the courage to do so. It should be noted that even if you're courageous, you may choose not to go for this task, if you simply don't like it. If such is the case, you may attempt many other risky tasks without issues. However if you lack courage, you may avoid engaging in all such tasks, where the element of risk is high.

However, risk is a necessary element and there may be no growth without it. Even the birth of an individual starts with a big risk, the risk which his mother takes by conceiving; even after knowing that such conception may cause many health problems. The same may also pose threat to her life. Medical science in the present times is advanced enough to make sure that in most cases, the mother as well as the baby is safe. However, when no medical science was there to start with, every mother took the risk of her health and life in order to bring life to existence.

They knew that greater achievements needed greater courage and accordingly, greater risks needed to be taken. Greater are the rewards, greater are the risks. The survival rate till the age of adulthood is low or very low among many species of animals, sea creatures, birds and other such species. Even then, their mothers conceive the babies and give birth to them, knowing well in advance that many of them will die. As these babies are born, many of them die young or very young and their mothers witness their deaths. Before you can even start to wonder, these mothers are ready to do it again.

The reason is that these species know that there are no rewards without risks, there is no success without failure and there is no life without death. Hence they only do what is required of them. They try to do so in the best possible ways by providing safe atmosphere to their new born babies; and they are then willing to take calculated amount of risk. No mother wants to see her babies die even if it is an animal or bird mother. However, they watch all such things and they keep giving birth after watching death again and again, as they know that there is no reward without risk.

Looking at the history of mankind, all great achievements have been accomplished with great risks. Hence if you have the negative habit of taking no risk or taking little risk, you should try and get rid of it. In order to do so, you need to replace the script of 'I don't want to lose or get hurt' with 'I'm fine if I lose or get hurt'; on your subconscious mind. In order to do so, you need to engage in conscious acts of courage. As courage gets in, lack of courage has to get out.

Let's look at some practices which can help you getting rid of this habit. Start engaging in activities which involve small amounts of risk and which are not difficult. This is the first level and you shouldn't take big risks here since you may end up quitting as you suffer losses. As you move ahead, you may succeed at some of these activities and you may fail at some. However through the process, you may learn that even failures don't make you less as a person and they make you stronger.

Unlike in cases of many other habits, you don't need to win again and again in order to get rid of lack of courage. Your job is to attempt risky tasks, give them your best and not bother about the outcomes. Once you do so, your job is done. Hence you should not aim for success and you should be focused on attempts. As you do that again and again, your conscious mind sends signals to your subconscious to the effect, 'I can take risks'.

It should be noted that you are not looking for a message like 'I can take risks and win'. This message is focused more on winning and less on taking risks. Hence if you lose more than you win, you may end up quitting. Therefore, focus on 'I can take risks'. It means you should not bother whether you win or not.

Though you should try to succeed in all such activities, losing at many of them may help you more. The root cause of this problem is the fear that if you engage in risky activities; you may face failures, defeats and/or losses. Hence when you engage in such activities and you win or succeed in most of them, your fear may get weaker. When that happens, you may think you're getting better but you may not be. This is because you're dependent on outward results and not on yourself. Hence as you start losing, you may start having such fears again. Being human, everyone has to lose; less at times and more at times.

Real courage doesn't lie in taking risk when you are already certain of your success or victory. This is because there is no risk if you are sure to achieve success or victory. Real courage lies in taking risk even though it may be well calculated risk; and giving it your best whether you succeed or not. If latter is the case which means that you fail, accept that failure and try harder and smarter next time. Trying something and giving it your best is all you need to do and you should not worry about the outcomes. Every failure may teach you an important lesson.

Success can't teach us much and it is the failures that teach us the most important lessons of our lives. Once you've fallen into a pit, you may always be careful about it. Hence you may not fall into it again. Therefore, failures should be more welcome than successes as failures may not only teach you how to succeed but they may also teach how to maintain success once achieved, which success alone may never teach. This is because you may have failed many times to understand how not to fail.

Hence try risky tasks and fail at some of them. With each one of these small failures and losses, you may realize that you're still the same person or even stronger. It means you can move ahead with your life even if you fail, at times with even more strength. This is because if the worst can't shake you, what else can. Hence the best way to get rid of any fear is to face it. When it has done the worst it can to do to you and you still stand your ground; such fear has nothing more left to do. Hence it may leave you for good.

Looking at activities for the first level, choose some activities which you were afraid to do during your childhood and start attempting them now. This is because the fears which capture your mind during childhood are the foundations of all other fears of the same types which grow in the later years of your life. For this reason, shake this problem from its foundations.

Hence start this practice with such activities from your childhood which may not be difficult now but which still include elements of risk. The primary objective is to attempt these activities without bothering about winning or losing. As you engage in such activities, you may start having fun. At the same time, you may realize that losing is not as bad as you thought.

Taking an example, if you're afraid of football due to fear of losing, start playing it. You may lose a lot but such losses may not make you less as a person and they may make you more. With time, you may witness improvement also. Even if you see an improvement of 10% after a month or two, you have achieved two good things. You're better at the game now and you're not afraid of losing. It means one of your fears has left you for good.

Likewise, if you're a bad dancer, start taking dance classes or practice on your own. Though you may do poorly in the beginning, you may realize that such failures don't take anything away from you. Hence stick to the routines. With time, you may improve as a dancer and your fear of dancing may also leave you.

Looking at some physically and/or mentally risky activities, you may start to learn swimming, horse riding, driving a car or a heavy vehicle, climbing trees; or you can choose to visit deserted places. The activities which will help you the most are the ones you fear the most. Hence if horse riding is your worst fear, you may not gain much by learning how to swim if swimming doesn't scare you to start with.

Therefore, you should choose activities which you fear and which are easy at the same time. You can choose a number of other activities, depending on your fears. As you continue doing so, your conscious mind sends more and more messages to your subconscious to the effect, 'I'm fine if I lose or get hurt'.

Once you're comfortable with this level, move on to the next level and try things which are riskier. Move slowly and don't take such risks at any stage, which are far bigger than you can accommodate. With time and efforts, you may build resistance to fears and losses. Hence you may be able to try things which are duly risky. You may win at times and you may lose at times. However, you may realize that winning as well as losing is secondary; and playing is primary. Once you've reached this stage, all you may have is courage.

Looking at some helpful tips, try and learn from your failures as they are the best teachers. Observe each failure and try to find out what went wrong. The primary focus here is not on wining more but learning to improve. As you improve, you'll surely win more. However, improvement and not success should be your primary objective. Improvement is inner quality which doesn't depend on circumstances outside. Hence you should go for it. Success is an outward expression and it depends on a number of factors.

You may be the best in a sphere but you may still lose at times. Hence don't focus on success and focus on improvement. Memorize this fact that you can always improve but you can't always succeed. This is because you don't need outside factors to improve and all that matters is you. Success on the other hand is something you can't control. Hence don't bet on it.

It is interesting that more you improve, more you may succeed. However, the converse is not true. It means more success doesn't mean more improvement. Therefore, success may come as a result of improvement but improvement may not follow as a result of success. It is like a star can create light but the light can't create the star. Hence work on improvement and don't bother about success as it is bound to follow, like light is bound to be there with a star.

Looking at another tip, don't end up developing a habit of taking too many unnecessary risks; while trying to get out of lack of courage. Mark your boundaries well and always know how much is too much. Risks are worthy of being taken when they are necessary or they offer required growth in various spheres of life. However, you should stay away from them if you wish to engage in them merely for fun, as such practices may turn into the habit of taking too many risks.

Taking an example, it is wise to fight with someone stronger than you, if he's trying to hurt someone you care for. However, it is not wise to mess with the same person, merely for fun. Though the risk of getting hurt is involved in both the cases, it is necessary in the first case whereas it is unnecessary in the second case. Hence be wise enough to make this distinction.

Making Excuses

One more negative trait which can cause problems is the habit of making excuses instead of doing your job properly and admitting your mistakes when you fail to do so.

Some people don't do what is required of them in various spheres, in proper and/or timely manner. When the other person objects, one such person may make excuses and he may give many justifications for the problem at hand, instead of admitting his mistake. Though he may think he has fooled the other person with such excuses, he may only add fuel to the fire in most cases.

Everyone can face such situations from time to time when circumstances may not allow to complete certain tasks in proper and/or timely manner. This much should be fine. However, if you have developed a habit of not doing your tasks properly and then make excuses, it can cause serious concerns. Slowly but surely, you will lose credibility and most people may avoid giving you important tasks. This is because you're not dependable.

Hence you need to fix this habit. Let's look at the root cause of this habit. This problem initiated when at a point in time; you couldn't complete a task at hand in proper/timely manner. Due to fear of loss or humiliation, you consciously chose to make excuses, instead of admitting your mistakes. The other person believed you since there was no reason for not believing you at that time. Hence you were saved. This encouraged you that if you can save yourself from apologies and/or punishments by making excuses, why not do so instead of admitting your mistakes.

Hence you tried it again and it worked. This gave more encouragement and you tried it again and again. Such conscious acts of making excuses wrote a script of 'make excuses instead of admitting mistakes'; on your subconscious mind, with time and repetition. When that happened, you started making excuses without any conscious effort, which means naturally, which means subconsciously.

This habit was carried forward to your present life like all other habits and you started having it from the beginning. Hence you choose to make excuses instead of apologizing when a task is not completed because of your ignorance or mistakes. In the beginning, most people may believe you since they may not think you're lying. However with time and repetition, they may understand that you have a habit of not completing tasks in proper/timely manner and then make excuses. This is when people start avoiding you.

Another aspect of this problem is that you may not bother completing your tasks in proper/timely manner. This is because you know you can make excuses. Hence this habit affects your performance, more and more with time. It means that people not trusting you is a smaller problem in comparison to you choosing not to complete tasks in proper/timely manner. This is because if you're able to complete your tasks properly, you don't need to make excuses.

Hence the habit of not completing your tasks in proper/timely manner may also come in combination with the habit of making excuses. One habit feeds the other and they may both get aggravated. You make excuses because you don't deliver and you don't deliver because you know you can make excuses.

Hence you need to change both these habits and you should start with the habit of making excuses. Though it may seem that you should fix the habit of not delivering results first as that may fix the need to make excuses, doing so is not the best way to deal with this problem. Understand that you have developed a habit of making excuses over a period of time. Hence if you treat and cure your problem of not delivering in proper/timely manner, you may not need to make excuses and both your problems may seem to go away.

In reality, you may only get rid of one habit, that of not delivering in proper/timely manner. When it comes to the habit of making excuses, you have not got rid of it. It is very much there but you don't get opportunities to engage in it. Not having a habit and not being able to express despite having it are two different aspects. In the second case, you do have the habit but the opportunity to express is not there. The moment an opportunity arises, the habit may express. The catch is that as long as a habit is there, it'll almost always create opportunities.

Hence as long as the habit of making excuses is there, you may not be able to fix the habit of not completing your tasks in proper/timely manner. It is like you choose to settle in a city or state where selling and consuming liquor is prohibited, in order to get rid of your habit of drinking too much. Though you may think you've got rid of the problem with time, you have not. This is because the urge may still be there and only the opportunities have disappeared. The moment an opportunity appears, the urge may take over again.

Hence you have quitted alcohol properly, only if you have all the opportunities to consume it but you don't want to. Likewise, you can't call yourself honest if you've not come across any opportunity which offered you to engage in an act of corruption on a large scale. It means if you can reject millions of dollars or other big temptations in exchange for engaging in acts of corruption; you may be honest. However if you don't get such chances, you may or may not be honest.

Just like the presence of liquor is the test whether or not you've quitted in the real sense, the presence of opportunities for corruption is the test whether or not you're honest. In the absence of opportunity, you may or may not have a habit. Hence the best way to test a habit or tendency is in the presence of extremely opposite circumstances.

Wood has a tendency to catch fire, stone/rock has a tendency not to catch fire whereas water has a tendency to pacify fire. However, in the absence of fire, all of them seem to behave the same; which means unaffected by fire. It is only when they interact with fire that their true natures will be revealed. As that happens, wood may catch fire, stone/rock may stay unaffected and water may try to extinguish fire.

A piece of wood can be there without catching fire for a 100 years or more. However, it doesn't mean it won't catch fire. It means that it never came in contact with fire. Hence this piece of wood is not immune to fire, it is lucky not to have come in contact with fire. Virtue is true only if it can sustain in the worst possible circumstances.

When it comes to negative habits, the best way to get rid of them is by developing immunity to them; and not by removing the opportunities to engage in them. Though the second practice may provide some temporary relief and it may be used in the beginning stages; it is not a permanent fix. Hence focus on the habit of making excuses. Once you've fixed it, you don't want to make excuses, instead of not having the opportunities to make excuses. It means your problem has been fixed properly since you've become immune to making excuses.

As always, it may take long to change a habit. Subconscious may be considered like an ocean. Even if you wish to raise its temperature only by 1 degree, it may take long. Likewise, if you wish to reduce its temperature only by 1 degree, it may take long. In the same way, it may take long to write a script/habit on the subconscious and it may take long to replace it with another script/habit.

The subconscious is a creature of habit and one of its jobs is to execute such commands on behalf of the conscious, which are required on regular basis. This practice reduces load on the conscious mind, thereby reducing the load on the entire system. For the same task, you may need 10 times less effort when doing it subconsciously, compared to when doing it consciously. Hence the subconscious reduces the load on the system and it saves energy.

This is why you may get accustomed to various types of keyboards and keypads of various gadgets with time. With practice, your fingers may automatically seem to press the keys that you wish to press. This is because your subconscious mind has recorded all the movements and it performs this operation for you. Since you can't feel the actions of the subconscious, you may feel like you're typing naturally.

Change your keyboard type or get a new phone with a different type of keypad. You'll notice that you need to engage in conscious efforts in order to get accustomed to the new keyboard. This is because your subconscious knows that certain specific keys lie at certain specific places. Since the arrangement of keys has changed, you may keep typing wrong words as the subconscious may press J instead of K, since J lies where K lied. With conscious efforts and time, you need to tell your subconscious that K has a new position, along with many other alphabets and letters. Once the subconscious records the new script; you may start typing naturally on this keyboard also.

The same applies to all other spheres of life. Taking another example, you may need due conscious effort when you try to visit a place for the first time, since you don't know its exact location and you need to find it. Once you've visited such place 100 times or more, you may not have to think at all and your car may automatically take you there. This is because your subconscious has memorized the route through repetition. This is why you can keep talking on phone when you go to your office, since your subconscious is driving the car, most of the time.

However, you can't do the same when you're trying to find a place for the first time. You need to do all the effort with your conscious mind in this case, since your subconscious has no record of this place. Hence you can't afford to talk on phone while driving since you need to engage your conscious mind in finding such place, with its full ability. It should be noted that talking to someone is almost always a conscious act. This is because you don't know what the other person is going to say and your responses are based on what they say.

Hence you need conscious focus while talking to someone since people don't talk according to fixed scripts. It means you may have talked to someone 1000s of times but he may come up with something new each time. The word 'new' is the domain of the conscious whereas the word 'repetition' is the domain of the subconscious. Since most people don't repeat what they say at different points in time; you need conscious effort in order to talk to someone.

Coming back to the main topic, you need to get rid of habit of making excuses, in order to fix your problem properly. Let's look at some practices which may help. Each time you fail to accomplish a task in proper/timely manner, make sure you admit your mistakes and you don't make excuses. As always, you should begin with small activities and build up from there. This way, your subconscious may not pose strong resistance because you're not undertaking tasks which are in strong opposition to the subconscious. It means you'll attempt tasks which are somewhat difficult but not a lot difficult than you can attempt at any point in time. The resistance won't be much in such cases and you may get through with conscious efforts.

The biggest hurdle as well as the biggest advantage on this path is your ego. Looking at the first aspect, your ego may make it very difficult for you to admit mistakes and apologize to people; since ego hates admitting mistakes and apologizing. Hence the best way to begin this practice is by admitting your mistakes to yourself. There are two benefits in this. Firstly, you may find it much easier to admit your mistakes to yourself than admitting them to other people.

Secondly and more importantly, you don't know how other people may react when you admit mistakes. One person may appreciate your gesture of being honest about your mistakes whereas another one may humiliate or even punish you for your mistakes. If the latter happens, it may discourage you and you may wish to disengage from the entire practice. Hence it's better to start on your own.

However, such acts need to be conscious as otherwise, they may not bring about changes. Hence try to make them as conscious as you can. For example, each time you fail to deliver, write or type 5 to 10 times that it's your mistake and you won't repeat it. While doing so, try to consciously engage as much as you can.

Apart from that, you can stand in front of mirror and address the person in the mirror as third party. Say in a fairly high volume to yourself that it is your mistake and you'll not repeat it. Be completely involved and treat yourself as you're treating a third person who's committed a mistake. Verbal admission is more difficult than written admission. Hence you may not need to repeat it 10 times like in case of written admission. For this reason, verbal admission with a graphic image of yourself in the mirror can prove very helpful, provided you're doing it seriously and not considering it some type of game.

You may have seen in some movies that if someone wishes to admit or confess something difficult, he or she writes a message instead of engaging in verbal admission or confession. This is because verbal admissions are more difficult than written ones. Even if the other person is not in front of you and you're to deliver such admission over phone, you may find it more difficult than dropping a message. Even when it comes to message, you may find that it is easier to type a message than recording a voice message. When you speak, your entire existence backs up this act, much more than it backs up the act of writing. Hence you're more aware and you need more conscious effort. Therefore, verbal admissions of mistakes are probably the best ones.

Once you've become comfortable with this level, you need to move to the second and more important level. At this stage, choose some people who may be only 1 or 2; who you trust and who you know are positive in general. Each time you commit one such mistake, admit it to them and assure them that you won't repeat it. For example, if you failed to deliver a product or item on time due to your ignorance, admit it to them in the evening or whenever you as well as they have time to spare, at the earliest. Doing so is a step forward since it is difficult to admit mistakes before other people. However, it may not be too much since you trust these people and you know they won't judge you unfairly.

Once you engage in such admissions, you may use your ego positively. Ego hates apologizing. Hence it may take two major paths to avoid this course of action. The first one is by making excuses and the second one is by making sure that you don't engage in such acts which result in you apologizing. Since you've eliminated the first path; it has to take the second path.

As a result, you may realize that you have started putting much more conscious effort to make sure that you don't repeat the same mistakes. This is because you have to admit them to such people again; that you failed despite promising not to fail. Hence your ego may do its best not to let that happen. Ego is the second most powerful entity lying within you; where the first one is the conscience. If you're smart, you can use your ego to your advantage. At this level, you may witness significant improvements.

You can build up from here and you may start admitting your mistakes to the people who are supposed to suffer due to such mistakes, during the third level. Here again, admit those mistakes which may cause relatively small problems; and you may cover up for those ones which you know may offend other people a lot. This is the third level and bigger mistakes should be admitted during the fourth level.

Once you're comfortable with the third level, you can move to the fourth level. Try to admit each and every one of your mistakes at this stage, no matter how big it may be. The beauty is that you may not commit many by the time you reach this stage. This is because with time and conscious efforts, you may have replaced the script on your subconscious mind from, 'why bother when you can make excuses' to 'better do your job properly than making excuses'. Hence you may complete most of your tasks in proper/timely manner. At this stage, you don't make many mistakes and you admit the ones you make. It means your habit of not completing tasks in proper/timely manner as well as that of making excuses is gone.

Along with this, start working on the habit of not completing tasks in proper/timely manner. Right from the first level, you should start putting conscious efforts on making sure that you complete your tasks properly. Assign yourself small but valuable tasks in the beginning and try to complete them properly.

Depending on your level of comfort, you may assign yourself various activities like, "from now on I will wake up 30, 20 or even 15 minutes earlier than I do", "I will clean my room on daily basis", "I will have lunch ready by 2 PM and dinner ready by 8:30 PM without fail", "I will wash or clean my car everyday between 7 AM and 8 AM or between any other specific times", "I will assist my wife in purchase of vegetables and I will do so in a proper and timely manner", I will go for a walk or for running every day or 3-4 times a week at a specific time and for a specific period of time", "I will read books offering knowledge for 15 or 30 minutes every day or for a couple of hours every week" and many other such tasks which you think may work best for you at this level.

As you start doing these activities again and again; your conscious mind will send more and more messages to your subconscious mind. These messages will say that you want to do your job in proper and timely manner and if you fail to do so, you are willing to admit your mistakes rather than making excuses. As these messages reach your subconscious mind again and again, they'll replace the old script and write a new one that you want.

Once you have mastered this level, move ahead and start applying this method to tasks in your professional sphere and other important spheres. With time and efforts, you may find that your subconscious mind is supporting you in doing so, instead of opposing you.

It was doing its job according to the old script earlier; and it is doing its job according to the new script now. Though it may seem to behave differently to you, it is doing the same job; executing the script written by your conscious mind, without any questions asked.

Hence choose wisely what you write on your subconscious mind because a right kind of script can make your subconscious your friend whereas a wrong kind of script can make it your enemy.

Excessive Aggression, Too Many Arguments

This enemy can take control of your mind for a short duration of time and it can make you say or do things which can cause damage. At times, this damage can be irreversible in nature.

It is the trait of having excessive aggression. This trait can spoil best of the things achieved by you and it can make people leave you though you may possess a number of good qualities. Hence you must get rid of excessive aggression if you have it.

Certain amount of aggression is needed in order to achieve your goals as without aggression, many goals may not be achieved. Hence aggression is not bad in itself, not knowing how to channelize it is. Excessive aggression may not stop you from achieving many of the big thing in life, but it may cause problems when it comes to sustain them. It can especially cause serious damage in the sphere of relationships as your dear ones may leave you or move away from you due to this trait. Hence you need to work on it.

Let's look at the root cause of this problem. We all have aggression though some people may have more than average and some may have less than average of it. Some may be good at channelizing aggression through various practices whereas some others may not know how to channelize it.

People who can channelize aggression in proper ways may achieve a lot in their lives since aggression is a very helpful quality if you wish to achieve success, especially in the sphere of profession. Majority of successful people have more or much more than average amount of aggression. However, they know how to tame and channelize such aggression. Hence they are able to control aggression instead of letting it control them.

People who can't control aggression may suffer from the problem of excessive aggression. Such aggression may come out in the form of physical or mental aggression from time to time. It may keep building inside one such person and when he's not able to control it any longer, it may burst out like lava from a volcano. Hence this problem has its root in having excessive physical and/or mental energy and not knowing what to do with such energy.

Depending on which type of energy is in excess, the outcomes may vary. People who have excessive physical aggression may often express it in the form of physical activities like fighting with other people, throwing things around, hitting other people and things or even hitting themselves. People who have excessive mental aggression may often express it verbally and not physically. Hence it may come out in the form of too many arguments, heated arguments, complaints, accusations and other such things.

Therefore, in order to treat this problem, you first need to learn which type of excessive aggression you have, if you have it. Considering physical aggression first, you need to find ways to release excessive physical energy so that it doesn't bother you. Engaging in physically demanding activities is the best way to do so. Through such practices, you may release the extra energy on daily basis and there may not be any buildups.

Majority of successful people don't suffer from excessive physical aggression. This is because their jobs are so demanding that they consume all the extra energy they have. In fact, it is partly due to such extra physical energy that they are able to achieve so much. For example, take away that extra physical energy from a sportsman, politician, actor or a businessman and he may not be able to achieve the same amount of success, even if the rest of his abilities remain the same.

Looking at some activities, you may engage in activities like running, mountain climbing, cycling, playing football, tennis, swimming and many other physical activities which give you opportunities to release physical energy. You should choose to engage in those physical activities which you find yourself the most comfortable with.

Make sure that you don't engage in any type of physical activity which builds more and more muscle in your body. It means you should avoid doing much weight training as such training may increase the intensity of your problem. This is because when you engage in weight training, you start building more and more muscle. Hence more and more physical energy is stored in your body, in the form of extra muscle that your body is gaining. As you have more physical energy available, you may need to find more ways to release this extra energy. Since you are already suffering from excessive physical energy, inviting more physical energy to your body is not advisable.

Hence engage in physical activities where you don't gain much extra muscle. However, if you are a diehard fan of weight training and you feel very comfortable with it, you should mark some boundaries for your gym training. Plan your gym training in a way that you don't gain muscle beyond a certain point. Such point should be reasonable and you should not aim for a lot of extra muscle.

Looking at verbal aggression, you should engage in activities which help you release excessive mental aggression. You may choose to engage in activities like writing articles, books, poetry or songs; painting, singing, acting, dancing, giving advice to people, motivating others, crossword puzzles and other puzzles, video games and other types of games or activities which require mental effort. Apart from them, you may engage in a wide variety of other activities which give outward expression to mental energy. Engage in activities that you like the most and you may start feeling relaxed.

In the beginning, you should not engage in such practices which bring aggressive mental energy to you. Hence don't read many books which offer more and more information or the ones which are dramatic, dark or serious. Instead, go for books falling in the genres of comedy, romance (comic and not tragic) and inspiration. Such books may send in energies which may be the opposites of the ones you have. Hence they may counteract such energies and you may feel relieved. On the other hand, a murder mystery, a book filled with violence, a mentally or emotionally disturbing book or a sad book may send in energies which may be similar to the ones you already have. Hence such energies may aggravate your problems.

When it comes to books which offer knowledge, you should choose selectively. In the beginning, try to avoid as many of them as you can. Only use those ones which offer knowledge related to your profession or other important spheres of your life. Avoid books which offer knowledge related to the spheres which don't have anything to do with you at this time. This is because more knowledge means more mental energy. Hence such books may provide you with more fuel in the form of knowledge. It means you may hold your arguments longer now, since you have gained access to a number of new facts. Hence stay away from such books until you have reached third or fourth level where you may handle the energies of such books.

Watching movies and television programs which fall in the genres of comedy, music and romance (not tragic love stories) may also help, due to similar reasons as those for books. Such movies or programs may transfer such energies to you, which may counteract a number of such energies in your aura, which cause mental aggression. Among these genres, comedy may prove very helpful during all levels.

This is because majority of comedy movies, programs and books don't feature much logic and comedy is mostly without logic or reason. Logic is a serious thing and comedy is as light as it gets. Hence such programs make you laugh without much logic and this practice helps. The energy of these programs sends messages to your subconscious that you can laugh and be happy without logic or reason. As that happens again and again; you may start believing less in logic and more in the moment.

Since most arguments need logic in order to sustain, you may witness reduction in your tendency to engage in arguments. This is because you've started paying less attention to logic deep down, which means subconsciously. Apart from that, you may start enjoying a number of such things or situations around you, which don't seem to have much logic but which are good. As a collective result of these factors, you may witness reduction in mental aggression.

Musical programs, music videos or plain music have similar effect on your mind. They tend to counteract negative mental energies by trying to relax you, though they may not be as effective as comedy programs; especially during the beginning levels. Drama shows and daily soaps may be the worst ones to watch. This is because most of them are full of negativity, scheming, plotting, cheating, conspiracies and other negative activities.

Accordingly, these shows may send more and more aggressive mental energy to your mind and your problem may intensify. Therefore, you should stay away from such programs which send aggressive mental energy to your mind instead of sending energies which may pacify mental aggression.

To summarize, you should engage in activities which offer outward expression of physical/mental energy, depending on the type you have in excess. At the same time, you should stay away from such activities which provide aggressive physical/mental energy. In case you have excessive mental energy, you may benefit through programs or books which offer comedy, music and comic but not tragic romance.

Being Dishonest, Being Selfish

The negative habits of being dishonest, selfish, unkind, uncaring and possessive; they all have a common root. They are caused because of assigning so much importance to yourself that you're not able to assess the feelings as well as value of others.

In other words, ego is the root cause of all these problems. As you become more and more focused on yourself, you start caring less and less for others. Hence you want to achieve and collect most good things and you don't wish to share them with anyone or with most people. With conscious efforts, you've written a script on your subconscious mind that you wish to collect all the people and things you like and in order to do so, you're willing to engage in unfair practices. Hence you become greedy, selfish and dishonest.

Selfishness lies in the root of greed and dishonesty. You don't need to be dishonest and you can't be greedy unless you're selfish. It is the desire to collect everything you like, which makes you greedy and dishonest. Collecting for yourself is an act of selfishness, when such collections are far beyond your basic needs. Hence selfishness is the root cause of these two problems.

Similarly, other problems like being uncaring, unkind and possessive have their roots in selfishness. For example, when you are unkind to someone, it is because you know that in order to be kind, you will have to lose something or let go of something that you own or possess, if such help demands resources. On the other hand if such an act requires physical help or guidance, the first thing that may come to your mind is "why should I help this person when there is nothing in it for me"? In the first case, you don't help others in order to save what you have whereas in the second case, you don't help others because you don't have anything to gain. Hence it's about you in both the cases.

Moving ahead, in order to care for someone, you need to be selfless and you need to think beyond your personal gains. This is something that a selfish person may never do. Likewise in case of being possessive, you must be selfish in order to possess things and especially people, even against their wishes.

Each of us may have to act selfish, dishonest, uncaring, unkind or possessive at times, due to various reasons. Though doing so may not be good, it may be acceptable. However, if you do such things on regular basis, it means you've turned these practices into habits. Hence you're engaging in them, not because you have to, but because you want to. In the first case, you may do so because of circumstances and not because you take joy in such practices. However in the second case, you do so because you like them.

Taking an example, suppose you as well as another person has been bitten by a venomous snake and you have antidote which is sufficient for one person only. You may save yourself instead of saving the other person and you may feel sorry for the other person. Though this act may be considered selfish, you didn't have much choice. Hence you didn't save this person because of limitation and not because you wanted him to die.

Suppose you as well as another person has been bitten by a venomous snake and you have antidote which is sufficient to save five people. Even then if you let the other person die as you want to save all of antidote for yourself; you're selfish. This time, you're not engaging in such act because you don't have any choice. You have a choice to save both of you but you instead choose to save you only. In this case, you may not feel sorry for the other person when he dies. This is because you don't care about him and that is why you let him die though you could save him easily.

Looking at another example, suppose people are dying of hunger and you have food or resources which may be sufficient for you and your family for a week or so. Hence you may choose not to share such food since you have fears that you and your family may not survive without this food for long. Though such act may be called selfish but it may not be something you want to do as you may feel sorry for such people.

Suppose people are dying of hunger and you have food or resources which may last for years. Even then if you choose not to share such resources with the needy, you're selfish by choice and not because of any fears or limitations. The only reason that you don't want to share may be that you don't care what happens to other people and you're concerned about yourself only.

Likewise, some people may be dishonest at times, more because of circumstances, than willingly. For example, you may be an honest person but you may tell a lie in order to save your son from a serious trouble. Though it is still an act of dishonesty; you're doing so not because you enjoy doing so but because you're worried for the wellbeing of your son. Hence this may not be an honest act but it doesn't make you a person who's dishonest by choice.

On the other hand, if you engage in acts of dishonesty on regular basis, in order to make more money or gain other advantages; you're dishonest by choice. Though you can manage well by being honest, you want to earn more and more; even if you have to be dishonest in order to do so. Hence you're dishonest by choice and not because of some fear, compulsion or circumstances.

Such negative habits may add more and more negative energy to your aura, as they may make you engage in karmas which may be bad or very bad. Apart from that, they may hinder your spiritual growth. Hence you need to get rid of these habits at the earliest.

Let's look at some practices which may help you get rid of these habits. Start engaging in small conscious acts of kindness and let go of your possessions in small quantities or amounts. At this level, attempt small tasks and don't try to engage in big ones as you may fail. For example, if according to your financial status, you're comfortable with donating USD 5 every day, start with this amount and don't donate USD 500 in one go, in a bout of motivation.

If you go for the second option, you may regret soon after doing so and you may choose to disengage from this practice. At the same time, you may start looking for ways to recover the money you've lost. Such ways are likely to be unfair since you're suffering from being dishonest and selfish. It means you may end up aggravating your problem instead of reducing it.

Hence start with small acts and then build up as you feel comfortable. When you do that, your subconscious mind may put resistance, which may be somewhat but not a lot stronger than what you can consciously handle. Hence you may get through with conscious efforts. Apart from donations, you may engage in other acts of kindness which are suitable according to your level.

It means you may offer physical or other types of help to needy people or organizations. If you have a lot of money and possessions, you should engage more in donations than in acts of other types of help. This is because there may be strong subconscious attachment to money and other valuables due to which, you've gathered so much. It means money is what makes you weak or selfish. Hence start giving it away.

This way, you'll deal with the problem in the best possible manner. If you can learn to let go of money and you can keep doing so for a significant period of time, you may stop bothering about collecting more and more of it. When that happens, you may not engage in acts of being dishonest or selfish, since you don't have much to gain through them now. This is because you may not feel like making more money through unfair means when you already know that you're not going to save it and you're going to donate it. Since the extra money is not going to stay with you, you may choose to earn through fair means only.

As you engage in more and more such acts, your conscious mind may send signals to your subconscious to the effect that you're willing to let go of your possessions, in order to help other people. With time, the subconscious may start paying attention to these messages and it may start making changes to the script written on it; which says you're selfish, greedy and dishonest.

Looking at another aspect of this practice, as you help people, they may transfer positive energy to your aura. At the same time, you may enjoy the feeling of joy that they have when your help brings them relief. All these factors may help you. With time and efforts, you may feel comfortable with this level as your subconscious may stop posing resistance to your acts of kindness. When that happens, move to the next level and increase the quantum of help. Be wise enough to assess how much money or help you can afford to offer at any point in time. Don't cross that line as that may cause problems for you.

With time and efforts, your subconscious may replace more parts of the old script with the new script. As a result, it may start encouraging you to help people, instead of posing resistance. At the same time, it may start posing resistance, whenever you try to engage in acts of being selfish and hurt other people. This is because the subconscious now recognizes you as a kind and considerate person. Hence it may not let you be selfish and greedy. The mathematical equation on it says that if you're going to donate your money to the needy; why earn it through unfair means in the first place? As a result, you may find it increasingly difficult to be selfish.

As you engage in more and more selfless acts of kindness, you may develop a taste or habit for them. It means you may start enjoying the happiness your acts bring to people. Once you become addicted to such happiness, you may not be able to render them sorrows through selfish deeds, even if you want to. When you reach such stage, your habit of being selfish is gone.

Two opposite habits can't stay strong at the same time, within you. Hence when kindness arrives, selfishness starts packing. Selfishness may keep reducing as kindness gains more and more strength. The sum total of two opposite habits or energies within you is always 100. It means if you are 80% selfish, you may be 20% kind. Likewise, if you're 80% kind, you may only be 20% selfish.

This is a very important fact which you can use to your advantage. When it comes to get rid of a habit, there are broadly two ways of doing so. You can start fighting such habit but it may not prove effective. Looking at the other way, you can try to develop the habit which lies exactly opposite to the habit in question. This may work wonderfully.

The first way is the way of destruction, as you try to destroy a habit. Hence it is a negative method. Apart from that, you're constantly focused on the habit that you wish to get rid of; which can make your job difficult. This is because your conscious focus provides more strength to whatever thing or habit has such conscious focus. It is like you feel strong urges to eat certain things that you're prohibited to eat for some reason. Your conscious focus shifts on such things and they become more desirable.

The second method is to develop another habit which may take care of the habit that you wish to get rid of. This method is constructive as you don't try to destroy anything but you try to develop something. Your focus is on developing a habit and such focus may make it easy for you to develop it. Since you're not focusing on the habit that you're trying to quit, you don't provide extra strength to such habit.

Hence it is better to develop a positive habit which is the opposite of a negative habit, whenever you have that choice. For instance, you should focus on being kind and you should not focus on not being selfish. As kindness develops, selfishness has to leave. The same holds true for other habits.

Looking at the two strongest entities living within us; don't try to get rid of ego; and simply focus on developing conscience. As the percentage of conscience within you increases, ego decreases in the same ratio. When conscience reaches 100%, ego is gone and you're liberated.

Your subconscious mind can be your best friend and it can also be your worst enemy. However, it is graceful enough not only to always give you this choice; but also to allow you to change your choice at any time, though that may need effort and time.

Hence make your choices wisely and make best use of your subconscious mind, if you wish to achieve more in your life and you wish to witness more spiritual growth.

Contact Details

Website

www.AstrologerPanditJi.com

Facebook:

https://www.facebook.com/HimanshuShangari

Email IDs:

himanshu1847-himanshushangari@yahoo.com

himanshu1847-astrologerpanditji@yahoo.com

himanshushangari1847@gmail.com